from *Pantyhose*
to **SPANDEX**
Writers on the Job Redux

from *Pantyhose*
to SPANDEX
Writers on the Job Redux

edited by Walter Cummins
& Thomas E. Kennedy

Serving
House
Books

From Pantyhose to Spandex:
Writers on the Job Redux

ISBN: 978-0-9977797-7-6

Cover design by Peter Selgin

Cover art by Letisia Cruz—marker, pen and ink on paper

Serving House Books logo by Barry Lereng Wilmont

Published by Serving House Books LLC

Copenhagen, Denmark, and Florham Park, NJ

www.servinghousebooks.com

Member of The Independent Book Publishers Association

First Serving House Books Edition 2017

CONTENTS

INTRODUCTION

When we got the idea for this anthology, it was a natural. We received the brilliant, thoughtful and laugh-provoking essay from Susann Cokal, "My Life in Pantyhose." It is about the period when a woman, to work in an office, had to wear pantyhose if she wanted to keep her job. We already had the brilliantly funny essay by Mike Aloisi, who made a good living dressing up like comic book superheroes, "My Life in Spandex." Two editors said to one another, we have to do a *Writers on the Job Redux.*

We had the many Series 2 essays of the on-line column on the various jobs a writer will take to earn money to subsist that we do for Mike Neff's webdelsol.com—"Writers on the Job" (WOTJ)—which preceded *The New Yorker*'s idea, in "On the Job," June 2017, by 15 years; but we couldn't fit all the essays into this volume, so we reluctantly had to omit some. The assumption of the column is every writer does writing and teaching, so we ruled those jobs out. All other jobs were valid, although teaching writing to maximum security prisoners and teaching corporate writing provided other situations than simply teaching.

This volume is the follow-up to the Hopewell Publications anthology we did in 2008. We wanted to wait ten years between WOTJs, but we aren't getting any younger—and we had the essays, eighteen of them.

From "My Life in Pantyhose" to "My Life in Spandex," there are sixteen essays in between, every one of which we wanted to put first, but the demands of pagination wouldn't permit. So, we hope the reader will treat each as primary, while there is a collective thought behind the arrangement.

The authors of *From Pantyhose to Spandex: Writers on the Job Redux* take you on a tour through a single night in a taxi in Copenhagen while listening to Mahler's Ninth, through the "Melancholy House" of a maximum security prison and assigning juvenile delinquents as their sentence to do the sentences of an essay, through a woman's decision to sell her eggs for five thousand dollars, through why the legendary jewelry store is called "Tiffany" rather than "Tiffany's," and on to a beach where forty-eight thousand pounds of lobster wait to be packed, moonlighting (a teacher's necessity), the sleepless night of a veterinary assistant, working as a babysitter/envelope stuffer/car-hop/Christmas ball saleswoman/ gas-pump attendant/and so much more (as one of our poets did in her hilarious essay, "Experience"), a day job as a bookseller, a translator, and even more ways of putting food on the table to feed the muses.

If they don't get paid, writers will write for free. Writing is an addiction, as the author of one essay notes. We will discomfit, distress, even degrade ourselves if only we can keep soul and body together to go on writing—to the discovery of what makes us tick.

As Dostoyevski wrote at the start of his writing life, "I involve myself with this mystery because I want to be a human being."

—The Editors

My Life in Pantyhose
A gal begins work in the 1980s

Susann Cokal

I used to counsel young women never to do two things, or not to do them in conjunction: 1. learn to type; 2. buy pantyhose.

From time to time it was necessary to do one or the other, but the combination meant you were practically assured a future as a secretary, which was fine if that was what you wanted to do. But being secretarial in the 1980s, when I started my work life, meant having to appear constantly cheerful (which I was not) and receptive to lewd comments by unsavory older men (which I was not) and perforce enduring makeovers from one's female bosses, which usually meant wearing their cast-off foot-warping heels and pussy-bow blouses and even makeup in colors they had rejected, in general feeling as full of self-esteem as on the days in junior high when the cheerleaders took one aside and launched into a long list of impossible beauty tips.

The decade was supposed to be a transitional time, one in which women were getting more power and older gender roles were on the wane, but pantyhose were part of a gal's power outfit, and pantyhose were oppressive, uncomfortable, expensive, and awkward. And forget about sisterhood—women used pantyhose to control each other, perhaps even more than men did. We were all conforming to some vague idea of masculine preference that might (might!) let us hold on to femininity while we entered the world of men's offices.

In the 1980s, if you worked with a typewriter you also had to wear the hose, which back then cost $2.50 a pair on a good day and typically lasted no more than forty-eight hours, if that. They inevitably snagged on something under one's desk or in the files one was collating and stapling. Then they developed a "run" that exposed a thin strip of your pallid leg skin and meant you had to throw them away, possibly skipping out on your lunch hour to buy a new pair—when $4.00 an hour was a dreamy kind of wage and still didn't cover much. For me, living in California, alone or with roommates, in college or grad school, made saving up for rent and tuition and a few cans of Campbell's soup (I was anorexic so I didn't need much)—a task both Herculean and Sisyphean. How was a girl supposed to afford pantyhose on top of it all?

Also, pantyhose are by nature awful. They cling to the skin like sweat, and they create a warm, moist nursery for yeast, bacterial, and viral infections. They flatten and accentuate any leg hairs even the most conscientious shaver has growing, so they require constant vigilance and a ridiculous amount of maintenance for something doomed to evanesce like Brigadoon, leaving lumps of fine-knit plastic in a landfill. They cannot be recycled, and manufacturing them sends toxins into the air.

But my main objection is a selfish one: They're uncomfortable and they send a signal I don't want to put out.

On the other side of the advice spectrum, an older woman told me during a performance review at a corporate job that I should "buy some business suits and wear them every day." The reason being that I should "dress for the job you want to have and be sure you are seen professionally."

I could respond only with a blank stare. When pantyhose cost a few dollars, a business suit cost around a hundred or two, and suits have to be dry cleaned, so the price per wear was always growing. I was just somebody's assistant. I didn't have money to buy a steak, let alone a suit other than the one I'd got on sale when I went in for the job interview.

That same woman reprimanded me shortly afterward, when she saw me wearing more durable, thick tights to work rather than pantyhose. "You're slipping!" she said.

1. Nothing beats a great pair.

At first, admittedly, pantyhose entered my life with a silky sheen of glamor. They were advertised on television, in commercials featuring happy career girls gleefully opening a Humpty-Dumpty plastic half-egg to pull out a pair of L'eggs (get it) and montage-contemplating a carefree night on the town or a day behind a well-organized desk where their equally happy male coworkers—bosses—stopped by with stacks of paper and admiring glances for the legs in the pantyhose, and then the girls went on those dream dates with the bosses and married them. Fantastic!

The jingle was an irresistible earworm, even for a nine-year-old: *Our L'eggs—fit your legs—they help you, they hold you—they NEVER LET YOU GO!*

And this was a good thing. (Incidentally, L'eggs is one of the brands for which Peggy Olson and Joan Harris designed campaigns on *Mad Men*, which says a lot about where L'eggs stand in the canon of cultural references.)

L'eggs came in several varieties. Skating star Peggy Fleming touted one line, Sheer Energy, saying it "massages, stimulates, and refreshes my legs"—and titillated TV watchers—*because*, as yet another commercial told us, *nothing beats a great pair of L'eggs.* Then there were Undie-L'eggs, which featured a tap-dancing Joyce DeWitt from *Three's Company*, expressing her relief at finding "real" panties and hose in one so that she avoided panty lines, apparently a major plague on the woman of the 1970s. Control-top varieties firmed up (sort of) a pesky little belly, and some pairs came with extra-fragile sheer toes that could be worn with sandals. Of course they all conformed so effortlessly to the leg that no one could ever compare the wearer's ankles to an elephant's, as happened to one unlucky TV mom who wore inferior pantyhose when she took her TV daughter to the zoo.

Pantyhose. To the zoo. Think about it.

I remember an even more alluring commercial, this one for the drably named Hanes brand. In the ad a glamorous woman sits in a train, probably speeding through Europe, definitely wearing a hat. Who is she? What is her career? No doubt something glamorous, probably a spy. And while the viewer figures that out, an equally glamorous man sits down across from her and openly appraises her legs, and a nasal soprano voice populates the soundtrack: *Gentlemen ... prefer HANES.*

So that was a gentleman? So we learned. Forget about the stimulating massages offered by the L'eggs line; we now wanted to please those gentlemen, the spies who might love us. If they preferred Hanes (obviously) they would prefer us, and we were so used to pleasing our parents and teachers (the bosses of an old-fashioned childhood) that we knew instinctively what our next life step would entail.

On the playgrounds of Southern California, my friends and I sang all the jingles in a never-ending run of musical theater. *Hanes*, we bellowed the shimmery bridge of promise, *will make you smooth and silky, shapely—sexy!* Just what every eleven-year-old wanted to be. Really.

That espionage ad was part of a series, especially catchy, some of which are posted on YouTube. Pantyhose prevailed again when a Suzie Wong–style spy stole secret plans, then eluded capture by reclining on a divan and crossing her legs: *The cool official was no fool, but he forgot one basic rule: Gentlemen ... prefer HANES.* And in case we were inclined to blame the poor guy for a lapse in judgment: *A man can overlook a lot when Ultra Sheer is in the plot—gentlemen* (everybody now!) ...

My favorite commercial features a young woman in a fluffy white dress dashing up a staircase: *When rushing to that special ball, remember underneath it all* ... A pair of stout elderly gents out of *Alice in Wonderland* or Kaiser Wilhelm's doomed court variously twitch their mustaches and lose their monocles (incensing a female companion their own age) as their eyes travel up the pretty girl's *smooth and silky, shapely—sexy!* gams. Near the end, as the camera dwells on a perplexed leg that has somehow dropped its bow-toed slipper and can't do anything but pose, *Problems seem to disappear when a charming prince is near*—and a young man holds up the shoe, because—yes—*gentlemen ... prefer HANES.*

In the late seventies and early eighties, Cinderella's slipper hardly mattered anymore; Cinderella's stockings were all. The ads had done their jobs.

At my junior high and high schools, for example, after my family was transplanted to the mountains of New Mexico, pantyhose were de rigueur anytime a girl put on a skirt. It was customary to wear a pair in "tan," never mind how poorly "tan" matched one's actual skin color elsewhere. I heard the popular girls debating, and "tan" always came out on top; "taupe" was a distant second.

I was very pale, incapable of coaxing color to my skin no matter how long I "lay out" in the melanoma-inducing rays of high altitude. Getting my legs in a pair of pantyhose was especially important. My mother for some reason didn't even allow me to wear a bra, which was beyond social suicide, especially since I was large-chested and tended to pop out of everything. However, she did let me have a pair of her old pantyhose with a run in them, and some silvery nail polish with which to treat the edges of the run. So I went to school in a skirt, yes, with breasts wobbling about, and nail polish highlighting the flaw in my pantyhose.

Results were not pleasant. It would perhaps have been better to wear pachydermal socks at my ankles. But youth persisted in the face of parental laissez-faire: Grimly I wore the old pantyhose, and snagged more runs in them, and kept going. I had read an article in a major newspaper claiming that women felt naked without nylon on their legs; I was going to be a woman, so I had to feel the same way. I didn't expect to be beautiful—I have enormous teeth, for one thing, and the cheerleaders had informed me my hair was too thin—but I wanted to be … *appropriate.*

Another thing I wanted, at least as much as I wanted a bra and pantyhose of my own, was to take a typing class. Almost everybody had to in those years; we weren't born with keyboards fused to our wrists. I first taught myself when I was about ten, using a "Type Your Way Up!" manual at my elementary school; my first clocked speed was fifty words per minute. I took a class in high school and got up to ninety. I wanted to learn shorthand too, but my father wouldn't let me—"You're not going to be a secretary!" he shouted as if I'd done something nearly as bad as suggesting a career as a prostitute, which I did in fact suggest afterward, whereupon he told me seriously not to do it because those girls ended up with too many venereal diseases. Not just one venereal disease, *too many.*

A few years later, finally wearing a bra also cast off by my mother, whose chest was significantly smaller than mine and whose bras produced what's now called a muffin top—but more importantly, *without panty-hose*—I walked past a group of high school mean girls and heard them stage-whisper, "GROSS." And a shocked, "She's not wearing any hose!"

It's true. I wasn't. I'd given up that fight. And I didn't have to wear any at my first job, which was at Baskin-Robbins, scooping ice cream in a polyester shirt and long pants. It paid $2.50 an hour, well below minimum, but there was a loophole in New Mexico law that said a franchise owner could pay his retail employees as little as he wanted as long as everything he sold was made within state lines. Some of the youngest kids made $1.50.

I was at the top of Mr. Fitch's pay scale—Mr. Fitch, who said the teenaged workers were eating him blind and who had fascinatingly awful black hairs growing in the skin along the top of his nose.

I'll admit I was part of the problem, though I worked harder than most of the employees. Wildly bulimic at that point, I'd serve the customers, scrub the counters, eat a few spoonfuls, and retire to what we called the "little scoopers' room" to get rid of it all. This usually happened during the thunderstorms that came around three every afternoon and kept the customers away. If I didn't go out to dance in the rain, I was in the back room vomiting up Rocky Road. After a while, anytime I leaned forward (as if to scoop out a six-ounce dollop from a vaguely unsanitary, hoar-frosty tub), I started to throw up by reflex. I considered it a good thing. Ice cream is very easy to get rid of, which may be why I don't like it now; I've tasted it too many times.

I was significantly underweight, though not in a made-for-TV way. I still had big breasts, which at that age were as embarrassing as they were theoretically attractive. It was hard to find clothes. I decided to embrace the idea of cast-off duds and did all my shopping at thrift stores, where I could buy beautiful vintage cocktail dresses with rhinestones and beads for four or five dollars each. I probably looked like a callgirl stuck in a time warp. I made some of my own clothes, too, on a sewing machine my mother had bought in 1972 and never used.

When I left for college, I used an hour's earnings to buy a brand-new pair of pantyhose and didn't need them. I was back in California; I went barefoot.

I could now type over a hundred words a minute, though, and had a keen sense of grammar. I never figured out how to say no to typing out papers for friends and classmates, free of charge. I'd look at flyers for typists who offered their services at a dollar a page, and I thought how lovely it would be to make money; but even more than that, I wanted to be loved.

2. *Elegance means more than clothes.*

"Where are you going dressed like that?"

"She works in an *office*. She always gets to look nice when she goes to work."

That was a couple of my roommates one summer, in a house near the uni, watching me take a single bite out of a piece of bread on which I was pacing myself. I put the bread away (one slice was good for two or three meals) and tugged up my pantyhose, which kept yitching out of position because they were sticking to the bottom of a ruffly green prairie skirt I'd made myself and didn't have a proper petticoat for. I was in fact going to work. Without makeup, without anything that could be called an actual hairstyle, but with pantyhose. So I looked "nice."

It was a summer job that paid a few cents above minimum wage: $4.50. That was the bare-bottom exacted by my parents if I was going to stay in California that summer instead of returning to New Mexico and Baskin-Robbins. I'd got the job while taking an overload of classes, and it seemed like a possible escape from exhaustion, or at least a change: receptionist at a "dynamic branch office of a diversified investment corporation." The corporate equivalent of Sheer Energy pantyhose, which would stimulate and refresh not just my tired legs but my soul as well.

I had no idea what that description meant, and neither did the people who worked there. I'd been hired because the secretary, a former Miss Oregon USA who was sleeping with a vice president from the home office in Texas (somehow all this stuff sounds so *wrong* when it's written down, but it was as glamorous as a "special ball" back then) and didn't want to sit at the front desk anymore. Hiring a receptionist was her way of getting a promotion, although the promotion meant retiring to an office without windows where she read magazines and sent things to her mother using the business's mailing accounts. She also took days off to think about her relationship with the man in Texas; the man in Texas himself would call me up himself long-distance and tell me that was what she was doing.

15

Or I might get a phone call from her that began, "Go into my office," and concluded with my driving out to her apartment with some cash, picking up her car after she'd abandoned it on an on-ramp, or bundling up some fabric with which I was going to make pillows for her sofa (I am also a near-pro-level seamstress; the prairie skirts were just a beginning).

All of this was okay, because there wasn't actually any business at that business. It wasn't diversified at all; the "executives" were supposed to cold-call people with money and invite them to invest in an oil well, but they didn't really feel like doing that. All of the "executives" were men who spent most of the day pitching quarters at a wall and calculating wins and losses by how close they bounced to some arcane target. I'm pretty sure it was a variation on a drinking game I never played at college.

The "branch president" sometimes sat at his desk and had me bring him things to sign, mostly so he could declare proudly, "This is what we call—president business," or "This is what we call—oil and gas business," even though I could see the papers had nothing to do with the oil well. He was kind of simpleminded; he'd got the job because an investor (the only investor) felt some obligation to the man's mother and had sunk a lot of money into the as-yet-imaginary well and insisted that "Donna's boy" get the job. Eventually they hired his brother, too, who was a former hairdresser and very creepy.

The "branch president" wasn't exactly creepy, but he did have an amazingly ill-fit toupee skating over a fringe of very dirty hair beneath, and it was hard not to stare. He liked to leave his office door open while he called up women who'd given him their real phone numbers on "office excursions" to the Del Mar racetrack—excursions in which I was not included because someone had to stay behind to answer phones and I wasn't legal drinking age—and I'd listen to him telling these women he had made millions of dollars investing in businesses like El Torito, a chain of reasonably priced sit-down Mexican restaurants, and that his mother never had to worry about money because she had "Sonny Boy" to look after her.

He'd say that one several times in a row, like an incantation: "Sonny Boy … Sonny Boy … I'm Sonny Boy!" He stared at me while he said it, presumably to gauge the effect he was having on the woman at the other end of the line.

It was all very amusing and pretty easy to ignore. I was a serious student. I would depart that August to spend my junior year at the university in Poitiers, France, so I studied vocabulary lists and tried to read the French canon. For fun, I also read *Anna Karenina* and all of Thomas Hardy. I had a typewriter at my station, an IBM Selectric (now that name sounds porny) and I used it to type out my thoughts about the books and to work on some short stories and a novel I'd begun when I was seventeen. I'm pretty sure that the main character in that novel wore white pantyhose, because those had been fashionable when I'd started writing.

The "executives" found my seriousness adorable. One said I was wholesome and invited me out to see *The Pope of Greenwich Village*. It was semi-tempting. I had a boyfriend who was interning at a biotech company nearby and mostly wanted to watch MTV at night, when it still showed music videos. The boyfriend was from a good middle-class family, which meant he liked pantyhose and prairie skirts. He thought I was too flabby, though, and pestered me to take jazz-dance classes, as if there were any way I could have eaten as little as I did and still manage to jump around in a leotard. When we went to the beach, he pulled on the strings of my bikini to make my boobs into marionettes that talked to each other.

A few weeks into my tenure at the diversified corporation, the secretary turned up, on time, with grocery bags full of things for me. Naturally these were not food items, as my self-starved body was doing okay as far as she could tell; she had brought me makeup and high heels and clothes she'd grown out of, having gained ten pounds since she took up with the Texan.

"We're doing a maaaakeoooooover!" she exclaimed happily, a word hard for me to understand as she burbled it and, no doubt, just as hard to make sense of in writing. She pulled me into the bathroom, phones be damned, and started painting my face with heavy kohl eyeliner, brown shadow, sparkly blush, red lipstick. In the end I had a face that was not really a face, the way I feel when looking at plastic surgery now.

"Well, that's better!" Miss Oregon said, and then she started tugging at my shoes. She said no self-respecting woman wore shoes less than three inches high, and the ones she was giving me were mostly what's called mules, just a thin strap across the front and nothing to hold them on behind. The heels got stuck when I pressed down the gas pedal of my VW squareback, which was sometimes frightening on the highways, and I tripped so often I became the object of office witticisms: "Have a nice trip, Susie—see you next fall!" and the like.

Wearing those shoes, I was over six feet tall, and falling down that much was a bad idea. I wrecked countless pairs of pantyhose. Nobody offered me new ones; pantyhose were my responsibility.

A little while later, the "branch president" told me quite seriously, "I have seen a hundred-percent improvement in you since DeeDee began helping you out."

The moment he judged me was the moment he became creepy too, but I had to say thanks; it was my job. It was also my job to let Miss Oregon send me to a beauty salon to get highlights put in my hair, and a real haircut. The streaks in my locks were freaky and made me cry, which made the crazy eyeliner run down my face, and I'm sure I sweated some more into the pantyhose (I feel as if I have to mention them here, as they are the governing metaphor of my work life).

Our L'eggs—fit your legs—they help you, they hold you . . .

Eventually I let them go. I made it to France, still with the makeup, and I wore pantyhose and some of those shoes in the hilly streets—for a short while. An American guy friend told me, "Man was not made to walk constantly downhill." I said, "Man may not have been, but woman reputedly was." It was received wisdom.

Nonetheless, I threw all those shoes away and wore my canvas sneakers everywhere. I also dyed my hair black, which went better with Miss Oregon's makeup, and I enjoyed being asked, "*Etes-vous japonaise?*" . . . but only in Paris, for some reason; in Paris I seemed Japanese, in Poitiers just a hulking pale American proto-goth.

French department stores had beautiful sections just for pantyhose and old-fashioned thigh-high stockings, organized by *deniers*—the scale of the knit they offered, from very sheer to very thick. Sometimes I went to look at them; seeing a large quantity of almost anything lovingly displayed is a powerful experience.

3. Massages, stimulates, and refreshes old fetishes.

When I returned to America in 1985, a revolution had taken place. My surf-and-science Southern California college now had a cardboard shantytown in protest of Apartheid. CDs were replacing vinyl records and even cassette tapes. And thigh-high stockings with visible garters were in vogue.

Strange as it sounds, one truth became indisputable: pantyhose were clearly an improvement over what had gone before. Try to imagine a thin, tight garter belt digging into your flesh and creeping downward or, god help us, garters attached to the bottom of an elastic or steel-boned girdle. They're medieval torture devices. The top of a stocking fits into a flat metal loop on the "shapewear," and then a rubber button slides up into a notch to hold the stockings in place.

Theoretically. They are always popping out, which is why you need two or four or six of them per leg. And, as I knew from reading novels set in the 1940s and 1950s, a gal had to be sure the seams in back were straight or she'd ruin the impression she made from behind.

Stockings and garters and girdles had never entirely vanished, of course, though they'd been temporarily eclipsed in what was at the time an efficiency culture, which was how hosiery evolved in the first place. Presumably the first stockings—even Caesar's army wore some kind of socks—were for warmth, not glamor. And the first iteration of pantyhose was made for showgirls around the 1920s, when costumers cleverly sewed long stockings to the girdles and bloomers of the gals kicking on stage or silver screen. The legs looked even-toned; the spotlight caressed them.

Showbiz or just biz or not, stockings might have become a casualty of World War II, as the silk from which they were made was diverted to the military; the army used the thread for parachutes. But the hose aesthetic endured. Some women tried dabbing their legs with foundation makeup to give the illusion … Oh, it was exhausting to think about the lengths to which they would go to look covered, smooth, and silky.

Then when Dior introduced the postwar New Look—basically a return to corsets and hoop skirts—everyone got lavish with textiles, and stockings were definitely back, often in nylon. There was, however, some dissatisfaction with the way they had to be worn, and the technology of the Cold War was brought to bear on women's legs. Scientists and designers noodled around with the idea of marketing practical "panties + hosiery" in the 1950s, often squabbling over who'd thought of some technique first. The idea didn't catch on in the epoch of corset/girdles and fluffy skirts, but Spandex and nylon grew stronger and springier, clingier and shinier, every year. The times they were a-changing, and the hosiers were ready.

The miniskirts of the 1960s at last made pantyhose "a necessity"—if not for hippies, at least for girls at work and school and parties (and moms going to the zoo). Whether sheer-to-the-waist or reinforced to the crotch, pantyhose provided double protection for an area subject to immodest exposure as a girl walked around, and avoided the bulges where a garter belt cut into the flesh and garters rippled.

All young women were showgirls then. My father once told me that in the 1960s, when he gave chemistry lectures in amphitheater-style halls, he got a complete anatomy lesson.

Incidentally, tampons hit big at the same time and for some of the same reasons—wearing a bulky pad, especially one that had to be pinned to a separate elastic belt, simply wouldn't work anymore.

Tampons meant freedom—and so, in those days, did pantyhose. Comparatively. In 1970, sales of pantyhose surpassed regular stockings.

I think now that in a culture of increasing liberation, hosiery of all types had become some kind of transitional object, like a child's blanket, reassuring the wearer that she belonged in her own skin and also in a larger society of hose-wearing females. Why else would twelve-year-old girls and seventy-year-old women alike feel such a strong need for them?

The old-fashioned stockings and garters endured as part of fetish culture, along with old Bettie Page pinups and *The Rocky Horror Picture Show*, which of course I'd seen and laughed at. What brought stockings and garters back into the mainstream circa 1985: Victoria's Secret took over American malls, and MTV had been showing garters in videos such as ZZ Top's "(She's Got) Legs" and John Cougar Mellencamp's "Hurts So Good," in which the singer wears a codpiece and struts around with models in fishnets and garters.

Suddenly everyone in San Diego was a fetishist. Everywhere I looked, garter belts and seamed stockings were striping the legs of giggling college girls. It hurt so good to be sexy, and this was what the gentlemen preferred now.

Not so many codpieces, though.

So yes, I got some. I had to. I was a pioneer of the goth/vintage look after all, at least by happenstance. The old/new-fashioned legwear was uncomfortable, but I gritted my teeth and bore the wee points of pain, which were especially bad when I sat down on the little rubber buttons and metal clasps. Then I got runs in all my stockings and with a sigh of relief went bare again.

4. *A man can overlook a lot.*

Springtime of my senior year, with a drawer full of laddered stockings (they were good for holding back my hair while I washed my face), saw my entrée into the publishing world—or so I thought it would. Entrée involved wearing pantyhose in the central library of my college, which was designed to look like a spaceship and has since been named after the real Doctor Seuss, Theodore Geisel. I went there to meet a published author, a psychologist with a book due out soon, who was in need of a personal assistant.

I wore one of my more cheerful thrift-store dresses, a green satin brocade with a paisley mixed in, and a pair of pantyhose, and some pointy green pumps my grandmother had given me, saying they had been my aunt's. The psychologist was twice my age and trying to position himself at the forefront of the just-forming men's movement. (He succeeded.) He was also breaking up with a woman with whom he'd been living for years, so after I got the job, he was prone to sudden dissolution into tears while I sat nonplussed, fingers poised over the keyboard of the Selectric in his at-home office, wondering what to do.

I had imagined this job would be glamorous. But I didn't even have to dress up for it; in fact I wore my worst clothes and made myself intentionally frumpy. Much of the time I was driving out to the local coffee shop to get his Thermos filled, or to a copy store to run off Xeroxes that he would study intently for quality. He seemed to see things in the spray of toner that I didn't, and photocopying one article to his satisfaction could take multiple trips to different copy shops.

He also saw a sea view from his office, which he'd built on the roof of the ranch-style house he was keeping in the breakup. The house was coincidentally just a few blocks from the one where my family had lived while I was in grade school.

He was so proud of that view. To be supportive, I said I could see it too, a dark strip along the horizon. If I tried hard enough, I really did see it.

His first priority at that time was arranging celebrity endorsements to adorn the jacket of his book-in-progress. He put a lot of thought into what those endorsements should be, and he did his best thinking on the toilet. During many of our hours together, he sat on the toilet and dictated what he called "fantasy quotes" to me, which I dutifully typed out on index cards just a foam-core door away.

Sometimes, after a particularly loud flatulation of the sort expected when a man is on the toilet, I was tempted to ask, "How do you want me to spell that?" But I didn't—because I was working for a *writer*, and that was a glamorous and good thing in itself.

And then there was his *movement*. Pun.

After each brainstorming session, we pored over the fantasy-quote index cards together, and he figured out which celebrity he wanted to ask to pretend to have said which superlative line. One of the fantasy quotes compared him to Copernicus; I remember suggesting he might aim slightly lower and invite the celebrity to come up with his/her own comparison. He winked and dimpled at me. He thought of himself as warm and wonderful.

The other big thing I know about that employer is that he'd spent years writing a book manuscript about incest—why families do it and why it can be good for them. He told me about it in some detail, and he explained that despite some celebrity endorsements already procured, he'd decided not to publish because putting that message out would ruin his career. Other people know about the book now, but I've read interviews in which he says that those who describe it as I've just done have misunderstood him. All I know is what he told me.

There was another reason I let myself go frumpy, beyond the already uncomfortable confluence of toilet and typewriter … Like most straight men back then, and perhaps in part because of his work on the oppression of males, this guy was a bit of a letch. He once had me bent down and wiggling to get to some books and files as we reorganized his office, and he said, "Woo-hoo, Cokal, looking sexy, hot stuff!"

To which I replied instinctively—as I would have answered any guy who said such a thing to me, "Fuck you."

I would never have predicted his next reaction: He burst into tears. I had, he told me, been hurtful.

Somehow I comforted him. Somehow I managed not to let that comfort involve sex. Honestly I don't think he considered me sexy at all anyway; he'd probably been throwing me a bone with the offensive remark.

At the same time I worked for the men's movement of one during the day, I had a pantyhose job at night. This time it was waitressing at Bob's Big Boy, which also required the girls to wear lipstick. I was a spectacularly bad waitress; I forgot to bring people the bread that came with their meals. They complained about it a lot. They also complained when I did bring the bread, as it was a wizened little roll pulled out of the freezer and set under the heat lamp for a few hours.

The uniform at Big Boy was a brown polyester dress and black shoes and, yes, pantyhose. I was living rent-free with my sister at our grandfather's old house, so theoretically I could afford to go to discount stores and buy "not first quality" pantyhose, inevitably destroyed each night. I was prone to nightmares and panics, and after going to bed at two I would sometimes wake up at four, convinced I had hot food waiting and knowing I was out of uniform, with cooks and customers angry at me. I would wake up all the way in front of the bathroom mirror, smearing on lipstick and fixing my hair and tugging on the treacherous hose and realizing that if I was there, I couldn't possibly need to be at Big Boy.

Part of my confusion, maybe, came from sleeping on the sofa. My sister and her ferret had claimed the only bedroom and she didn't have a job. Exposed as I was, I became the immediate target for the ferret whenever my sister opened her door. The ferret always seemed to want to bite someone or poop right by someone's head, and my sister thought it was hilarious. If I couldn't sleep after it woke me up, I read Barbara Pym novels and *The Name of the Rose* and hoped I'd find the courage to take my savings to Scotland or France and work as a waitress; Bob's Big Boy was supposed to be training for that working-class fantasy.

One Sunday afternoon—the writer didn't work on Sunday, and my Big Boy shift began at six—I went with a friend to the beach of my childhood. We were both in bikinis, of course. And of course there he was too. I want to say he was in a Speedo because that would be embarrassing for him, but he had on regular trunks. He came over to say hello. Later he asked me for my friend's number. He was reasonably good-looking for a guy twice our age, so she was flattered—but didn't want me to pass the number along.

She did run into him at medical school that fall, though, when he was giving a lecture to raise awareness about ways in which white men such as doctors had been oppressed through being the world's biggest wage earners. He said to her then, in front of her classmates, "I almost didn't recognize you with your clothes on!" She was mortified but also paradoxically proud; he was a real monocle-dropper.

By the time that happened, I had moved up the coast to grad school. I just couldn't take working the two jobs anymore, or the stench of my polyester Big Boy uniform at the end of a night, or the degradation of the "fantasy quotes" dictated from the toilet. Grad school was finally a more pleasant prospect. Berkeley did not seem like a pantyhose town.

5. *Heads will turn, you know it's true; all eyes can't help but notice you.*

Because I'd decided to go to grad school so late in the summer, I'd missed the deadline for a TAship, and I needed a job. I wore pantyhose to my interview with another psychologist, a female professor who had grant money to spend on a personal assistant. She smirked at the reputation of my last employer. Her own research involved roomfuls of undergrads gathered together as test subjects, listening to her taped voice reading off a list of nouns like "bluejay." Then they were supposed to make a chronological list of the nouns they'd heard. Unbeknownst to most of the group, there was one student, the "naysayer," who was told to disagree with them all and put the words into a different order. The study was about the power of saying no.

I spent a lonely year in which I felt *no* deep in my bones. I did become friends with one of the department secretaries, the one assigned specifically to my employer, and she—the secretary—agreed with me about the pernicious results of learning to type. She had a daughter she'd refused to allow to take typing classes. We all went to Jazzercize together. She gave me some of her cast-off clothes, which were more normal than mine, but she didn't offer them in an aggressive way; she just thought I might like them. She occasionally wore pantyhose but I didn't have to. Other secretaries in the department had stockings with seams, and they tugged at the garters from time to time as at badges of courage.

Midway through fall semester, the woman for whom I was working developed throat cancer and was forbidden to speak. Since she couldn't talk, there wasn't that much for me to do. I asked if she wanted to let me go and she wrote, "*No*," very emphatically. She got all her shouting out in writing. I tried to ooze positive energy, even when she forgot to sign my time cards and I didn't get paid.

One of the main things she wanted me to do was to buy her a new tape recorder with her grant money, even though she couldn't use the tape recorder because the doctors had predicted a lifetime of silence if she ever spoke. I called every electronics store in town while she sat at her desk and listened to me and shouted in writing. It turned out that the kind of tape recorder she wanted wasn't being made anymore, but she had a hard time accepting that. I provided her with lists of alternatives and typed up assessments of which store clerks and managers seemed most competent and helpful. She seemed to think this meant I was trying to sway her opinion unduly, and she shouted in a note, "*I* [underlined three times] *CHOOSE THE VENDOR.*"

I tried to explain I didn't have any problem with that but was trying to give her all the information. She wrote me that one reason I'd got the job over many other applicants was that I hadn't called myself a colleague, as one young man had done; I'd been aware all along that I was an assistant. She wrote that the best assistant she'd ever hired had been a housewife looking for something to do a few hours a week.

There were good aspects to the job too. I typed my papers on the typewriter in a tiny office upstairs. She really didn't have enough work for me. I got another job taking lecture notes for a professor who spoke very fast and wanted his students to have all the material. I wrote long letters to my best friend from high school, who wrote back, "Boring jobs with access to office equipment will keep our friendship strong."

They did. Thank god.

By the end of that dreadful year, I was ready to put the Ph.D. on hold for a while. I'd hooked up with the boy who'd TA'ed one of my anthropology classes as an undergrad, and we had a plan to backpack through Turkey and Europe.

When I quit, the psychologist was very nice about it. She told me—using her actual voice—"Be grateful that every day you have with this person is a day you didn't have before. And never do anything you don't want to do. Not even at work."

Which was weird, because I'd hated the job I'd had with her and because my next job involved pantyhose in a big way.

6. *(S)he forgot one basic rule.*

I moved back to San Diego—it always felt like home, and my then-boyfriend was still in grad school there—and worked as a Kelly temporary (Remember those? Skills tests asking whether it was okay to use paper clips in a file folder [according to them, it wasn't]) until an insurance brokerage wanted to hire me. The pansexual office manager (a female who loved boobs) and the gay male branch president told me they wanted to gaze at me at the front desk. The office manager asked me to wear a garter belt. I did, once in a while.

Mostly I sat at my desk, in pantyhose, and read novels and wrote in a notebook. It was not a well-run office; it seemed I'd been lucky again. Somehow the "executives" had managed to sell their reputation to the company headquarters in Anaheim, but neither of the "executives" was particularly motivated to sell anything else and the phones weren't ringing. So my job consisted mostly of an hour of filing in the morning and then seven hours of looking busy.

Well, there were one or two days of actual busyness. On one of those days, the office manager (who became my friend, especially after she told me about her "real" job, which was working as a sexual surrogate for men with Issues such as arrests for child molesting) wanted to go through all the files in the scant-shelved file room. I had a terrible sunburn from going to the beach that weekend, and each time I stood up to fetch another set of files, I thought I'd faint. But that was the worst thing I had to do there. Maybe it played to some sadistic streak in my friend, maybe not. The pantyhose I was wearing over the sunburn made me crazy with itching.

The branch manager, a decaying beauty of forty-two with bright red (dyed) hair and lips drawn way outside her natural lipline, decided to take me in hand. It was easier than doing actual work, as she was too shy to make the cold calls that would bring in business. One morning she walked in with grocery bags full of shoes and purses and skirts.

My heart sank. I knew what this meant. I'd been wearing my most "normal" clothes, and there were no clients to see me anyway, but once again I was going to get schooled in the art of elaborate makeup and plain business attire and shoes that hurt my feet.

I wore the stuff she gave me. I had to. For the record, I think I hate mules even more than I hate pantyhose.

In time the team hired another "executive" and the home office fired the gay one for not producing. We were three women and one straight man with a mustache who left the office with a newspaper at ten every morning, cocking the paper my direction and saying, "I'll be—right back." The words somehow made a plop in the air. I was glad there was no bathroom in the actual office because I didn't want to have to listen to him congratulating himself in it. Men complain about women's periods but I've never known a menstrual period that could compete with a dude's bowels for attention and interference in the workday.

There was once an occasion for taking photos—somebody's birthday, maybe—and the mustache man sat in a chair while the rest of us stood around him. It wasn't his birthday; I'm sure of that much. He wasn't even the branch "president" by then; the redhead was. But somebody decided it looked better for all the girls to be standing around the guy, who grinned as we teetered in our heels.

I told myself I didn't care. This wasn't going to be my career. I didn't even say anything when the mustache went off on a tear praising Oliver North as a national hero.

That office didn't have a bathroom but it did have a central "conversation area" surrounded by glass bricks. It was a nice place to eat the limp little sandwiches that were all my boyfriend and I could afford as we saved for an excursion to Turkey. He worked at night at the jail, evaluating prisoners to see if they could be released on their own recognizance, and he sometimes stopped by so we could see each other and share sandwiches. One day this almost got me fired, because when the "executives" returned from their lunch at Carl's Jr., the boyfriend and I stood up to greet them over the glass brick wall.

"If I was that girl's boss, I'd fire her ass," the mustache man said several times. I don't know who he thought *was* my boss, but the office manager informed me that what I'd done was very bad.

I did not know why.

"Two little heads popping up over the wall and saying hello," she said patiently.

I still didn't get it.

"Suze, you can't have sex in the office," she said—which was *really* confusing, not only because boyfriend and I had been fully clothed while eating our sandwiches on the sofa, but also because the stories I kept hearing from her involved everyone she'd ever worked with having sex with everyone else in an office, and then there was her other job too, the surrogate gig, and the fact that she'd told me she and her boyfriend fantasized about my boobs when they were shagging.

She still brought up that moment in the "conversation area" as if it was something I did wrong.

But to me the message back then was that if I was going to be blamed for having sex in the office I should actually do it, so the next time the "executives" went to Carl's Jr. for lunch … Yes, reader, the boyfriend and I did shag in the workplace. It was not on the sofa but in the kitchenette, on a laminate countertop. It was uncomfortable and it ripped a pair of pantyhose, but it proved a point, at least to us.

Later on, the redhead divorced her husband and married the mustache and also got a facelift.

I stayed friends with the office manager for years. She married someone she met through her "other job"—not a molester—and moved to a mountain.

28

My boyfriend and I went to Turkey, and in a cave in Cappadocia, a one-eyed man tried to pay money to have sex with me. My sweetheart was so upset about his failure to protect me that I had to comfort him and tell him everything was okay, when really of course it wasn't.

Somehow that feels like a pantyhose moment too. We broke up.

7. They help you; they hold you (back).

Somewhat adrift, I finished the Master's degree at Berkeley but I wasn't happy. I was still younger than anybody I knew in the program and I hated the competitiveness and general nasty attitudes my fellow-students had toward each other.

Naturally I decided that if I had to live with so much backbiting and politicking, I should do it in the corporate world, where it was all out in the open and nobody was pretending to be working for a greater good.

I applied for a pantyhose job.

The job was at a publishing house. I really, really wanted it. At the interview I said I believed that books could change the world.

With my spiffy c.v. and all my work experience and education, the one thing everyone commented on during the interview process was my typing speed. On the IBM Selectric I'd typed 120 wpm.

I wore a brand-new business suit to the interview, though the job was being an assistant to two young editors and they probably wondered why I had it on. I never used the padded rayon jacket again, though I sometimes put on the skirt. I had a few vintage 1960s suits, but a friend advised me to avoid standing out. I bought more normal thrift-store clothing, and I took the black out of my hair, and I wore the goddamn pantyhose. Though sometimes they were plaid or yellow (I'd bought those in Berkeley).

This was Real Publishing, the kind called a "glamour profession," punctuation and French u always implied, mostly because the term meant people wanted the jobs but weren't paid much to do them. Not much, but the most I'd made in my life till then: seventeen thousand a year. And five hundred on top. It was enough (barely) to pay rent on a studio apartment under the downtown flight path, and support me and a cat if I walked to work and never spent money on anything. But the beach was free, and I got to read books in the archives. Some of my favorite novels had come out of that publishing house in the 1950s and 60s.

The department where I worked was run almost entirely by women. In pantyhose. The only man working there was an editorial assistant who wore a Mickey Mouse watch and striped suspenders and said "at this time" a lot. He worked for the über-boss, who loved him— she raved about the watch and the suspenders and what a lot of "fun" he was. I liked him too; he was a very nice person; but I had to read and correct the grammar in what he wrote before he turned it in. I did that as a favor and sometimes he bought me a Greek salad.

I was also an editorial assistant, definitely unglamorous, and my job was to file and type and keep the books published on schedule.

This was easier with one of my supervisors than the other. The easy boss treated me as a secretary, which was what I was, while letting me give input on the manuscripts in her care. The less easy boss was uncomfortable with our proximity in age and the fact that one of my best friends had known her in her rah-rah college days, and she didn't delegate enough—she hated to tell me to file anything—so her filing piled up, and this reflected poorly on me.

The über-boss mostly worked at home or while flying around to see an aging musician for whom she was both fluffer and amanuensis. She was in the office a total of three days during my first three months, and one of those days coincided with the end of my probationary period. I was looking forward to being a fully fledged employee. After everyone had left that evening, she called me into her office and told me my probation would be extended because I wasn't measuring up.

Actually, she handed me a memo that told me that. The memo said I needed to improve in all areas but that my ability to take directions made her willing to take a risk on keeping me in the pool.

Despite the sofa scandal at the insurance brokerage, I had never been considered not-good at my job or unsatisfactory at anything I tried (admittedly, I had not tried hard to be a good waitress at Big Boy). The list of my sins was confusing: I needed to file things regularly, even if one editor didn't want me to; I needed to stop showing off, though I didn't know how I was doing it; I needed to use fewer big words and simplify my language on the phone because people thought I was acting snooty and waving around my M.A. from Berkeley. That last one was a shock because I never mentioned my degree and was ashamed of it because it wasn't a Ph.D. I thought everyone knew that if you left a Ph.D. program with only an M.A., even if you had a 4.0 GPA, you were either secretly stupid or else a loser who couldn't take the pressure.

While I sat in stunned silence, trying not to cry, she gave me the lecture about buying business suits. We talked a little. The Mickey Mouse watch got a mention—"What *fun!*"—but while my co-worker's watch was more than okay, my self-presentation was not.

The boss also told me that I needed to work on my confidence and on not letting myself seem weak in any way. She told me she'd once had to learn the same thing so that now, for example, she never let it appear as though she was having any trouble in her marriage.

I wondered why she was implicitly telling me she was having trouble in her marriage.

At the end of the conversation, I still had no idea how to improve my performance, other than the shopping spree I couldn't afford. So what I did was this: I stopped trying so hard to do a good job. I'd been going in at seven a.m. and leaving at six, skipping lunch, taking work to the library at Thanksgiving. With my probationary period extended, I started showing up when the office opened and taking a lunch break and leaving shortly after office hours were officially over. I suppose it was the equivalent of having sex at the office, but a miserable kind of sex. I read at home for pleasure and cried a lot and dated a mistake of a person who kept telling me I needed to get rid of that pout below my navel, which is there even when I weigh 120 pounds on a 5'9" frame and will these Californian men *please stop* commenting on it? He bought me dinners and thought it was natural that I went to the bathroom and threw them up again afterward. He had a connection to the job and said I was probably in trouble because everyone in the department wanted to date him but when he saw me he'd announced, "Make that girl go out with me." Which, he used to add when telling the story to his friends, the editors had done—they made me go out with him.

Actually, this wasn't true; I would have gone to dinner with him anyway, because the very first time I got a short story published in a magazine, he had been the illustrator, and therefore I connected him with glamor of the *gentlemen prefer* sort.

The über boss once used company funds to pay for that man and me to spend the night in a hotel room after an art show. She also took me shopping with her for a birthday present for him and told the sales clerk that she and I were sisters. I thought all this was odd behavior, but then again I'd also thought she approved of me up until the probation.

Yes, I recognize my mistakes … now. But back then I was tangled up in pantyhose and trying to be a good girl, a good employee, and somewhat happy with what I was doing. *Trying.* Anyway, the relationship—if it can be called that—ended fast.

A few days after the breakup, I got taken off probation. The über told me she'd seen "a night and day difference" in my performance and gave me a hug.

At that moment I officially hated her. I also hated myself and the system because it was such a mystery. I hated that the horrible man might have been right about sexual jealousy in a workplace I'd idealized for being a hive of feminine cooperation. (For the record, I don't think now that he actually was right, but I do know that was a miserable place to work.) I hated that this person who had been so critical of me and so stern saw herself as a beacon of hugging light. I hated that to be a woman in that environment, I had to let myself be hugged and pretend to like it. I hated the pantyhose sagging at my crotch and the way my legs felt hot and self-conscious during the hug.

Maybe my former employer, the fantasy-quote man, had had a point about the oppression suffered by white men. But there was also an oppression of women by women, and it wore a smile and a pair of L'eggs and claimed to belong to a sisterhood.

To this day, I don't believe my job performance had improved at all; in my depression, it had devolved, and I know my vocabulary suffered as I deliberately simplified it. I feel I'll never be as smart as I was before I had that job. But I suppose my ultimate reward was twofold—I got to work less hard and I also got accepted, at a level of mediocrity that made me more palatable to someone wearing pantyhose much spendier than mine.

The one thing I knew, really, was that I had to dress for a certain role. So I did. And I kept hating the clothes, the job, myself.

One night I almost died and when I went home after the hospital (and before the struggle over how to pay the bill with no insurance), I asked myself what I really wanted to do with my life. It did not involve pantyhose. I went back to grad school—on the other side of the continent, in a different discipline—and I racked up two Ph.D.'s while freelancing as a copyeditor and occasional book doctor for an editor (not in the circle mentioned above) who saw something in me and my work on all those stacks of manuscript, and who is now *my* editor, the publisher of my third and most successful novel.

I'm pretty sure she doesn't own a single pair of pantyhose or even stockings. She's British.

8. Problems seem to disappear ... ?

I'm trying to calculate, now, how many pairs of pantyhose I've owned in my life and how many I've discarded. I'm an at-home novelist and on-campus professor. I live in Virginia, where in summer I go bare and in winter I wear fishnet tights, which are durable and let the air circulate comfortably around one's legs but probably look like a misguided attempt at sexiness as I leave behind my fifth decade of living.

For years I haven't needed pantyhose at all, but as I noted parenthetically many pages ago, they are the governing metaphor of my early work life. I'm always uneasily aware of them. And I'm not alone in that; when a friend was invited to give a speech at graduation, she knew she should wear a skirt, but she had to ask around about whether pantyhose would be a required part of the outfit. She decided to err on the safe side and bought herself a pair of Calvin Kleins.

I'll leave other kinds of stockings out of the tally—but believe it or not, I've discovered that old-fashioned corsets often give an injured back some good support, and sometimes it's easiest to attach Dita Von Teese–type stockings and live with the little points of pain that have faded in comparison to chronic migraines. And there's always the possibility that one's veins will pop or diabetes will necessitate some kind of "compression hosiery" bought at medical warehouses.

As to pantyhose, I still have maybe a dozen pairs in a box somewhere, for emergency formal occasions and job interviews—but women aren't really wearing pantyhose to job interviews in academia anymore. They wear tights or pantsuits.

I still prefer skirts, and my wardrobe is at least fifty-percent vintage. I wore my college clothes well past tenure and into my forties, when my then-boyfriend (now my husband) took a look in my closet and said, "You might think of buying some stuff without holes or faded patches."

It made sense. I am now a professional woman, a term that has changed a lot since my twenties. I went on eBay and bought some high-quality thrift. I also gained some weight when I finally kicked bulimia, so I'm shopping again. But not for pantyhose.

Here's a rough figure: Say two or three pairs a week for the months and years I had pantyhose-typewriter jobs, and a few more pairs for interviews at jobs I either didn't get or didn't need pantyhose for … and remembering that even Bob's Big Boy required run-free pantyhose of its waitresses … I'm guessing the number to be around 370.

Three hundred and seventy.

That figure seems both high and low. I've spent years not wearing those maddening, snaggy, runny, expensive abominations to the female form and psyche, but mentally the pantyhose are always with me, even though I've been able to use my typing (145 wpm at last testing) for more than other persons' reports and forms and letters and papers.

I can't say I've enjoyed any job very much for long. I'm not much of an Organization person and I still have a tendency to drop a "Fuck you" if I feel pushed too hard, too inappropriately. If I were to go into administration, I'd have to curb my tongue and pull out the hose again; it's part of the culture. As is Spanx, and other "shapewear" that has become famously if wry-smirkily expected of women in the public sphere. Because of health issues and an innate drive toward solitude, I work at home as much as I can, and it's best not to describe what I wear then.

Pantyhose, surprisingly, have developed a flourishing fetish category of their own, often involving hose pulled over the head of an outwardly alpha man being tortured, and/or worn on the legs and pulled up so high they smash his wobbly bits. A dominatrix splits them open and he loves it. This kind of thing doesn't have its own category on PornHub.com yet, but I'm keeping my eyes peeled. White men oppressed by their success and ability to earn are said to eat this stuff up.

But back to me: Wherever I am, I'm always aware of pantyhose, and if I didn't have at least those few pairs in a drawer I'd be anxious. You never know when you're going to need them, that's the thing.

However women have managed to free themselves from the L'eggs that fit their legs, the hateful things are still sold (albeit on much smaller racks) in grocery stores in case we need to pick up a quick pair on the way to or from a special ball, or work, and now they cost seven or eight dollars. Designer brands can list at seventy or eighty a pair.

Really, why?

Here's the big rub: However we may twist our talents, whether we want to be secretaries (a profession for which I have great respect after all) or not, even if we've managed to rid ourselves of the stereotype of the perky office Girl Friday in her makeup and heels and hose, and although some workplaces actually do make an effort to eradicate the kind of sleazy male mustache-twitching that obtained during my pantyhose years in the 1980s and endures even now, one catchy fact holds true somewhere deep in our psyches, and it's almost what Ernest Hemingway said happens if you've been young and in Paris (and at a typewriter) …

If you've been young and in pantyhose, here's the truth: Whether they help you or hold you—

THEY NEVER LET YOU GO.

TESTIMONY OF A COPENHAGEN TAXIDRIVER
AN ESSAY IN FOUR MOVEMENTS

Per Šmidl

> "The thing is to swallow the real facts of your destiny, and
> then, there you are."
> —Vincent Van Gogh

1.

"It's just a short ride!" he booms as he swings into the front passenger seat of the cab. Giving me his hand, he says, "Hey! You reek of garlic. My name's Magnus!"

"Uh-huh, and you reek of booze. My name's Per." I give his hand a good squeeze. "But tell me! Does Magnus know where he wants to go?"

Magnus leans back and his face takes on an amused expression, as he says: "Magnus wants to go to Bodenhoff Square."

I nod and pull out into the middle of the road.

"I sure am Magnus," Magnus muses "and you sure are Per. And here we are. Magnus and Per have met each other for the first time in their lives. Isn't that just... GREAT!"

I declare that it sure is high time we finally met. "Magnus," I moan, "where have you been all these years?" In response Magnus raises his right hand and wants to give me high five. I raise mine back.

"Hoo-ee!" he yells as our palms slap. At that moment he seems not only drunk but very happy.

During the three-four minutes it takes me to bring Magnus to Bodenhoff Square we manage to become great buddies; we laugh into each others' faces and give each other high five probably eight times. "Hey man, this is too funny!" Magnus hollers. And I totally agree. It really is a jolly ride. Only trouble is when it is time for the two new buddies to part breaking the bond is more than we can bear. Still, after another five or six minutes (and as many high fives) we finally succeed in disengaging from each other.

And as I drive on, it is with the pleasurable feeling that I really earned the handsome tip Magnus left me in the cash I so cherish. Feeling almost high, I am on my way towards the next customer and, who knows, the next adventure.

The tires of the Mercedes cab rumble along the cobblestones of the street next to Christianshavns Canal in Copenhagen. The time is just after nine pm. It is the slow spell of an ordinary evening towards the end of winter. The antique black lampposts throw feeble yellowish light, and from the speakers sound the opening notes of what is tonight's concert on Denmark's radio: the *andante comodo* first movement of Gustav Mahler's Ninth Symphony. I feel a calm coming over me and listen. The empty car no longer feels quite as empty as it did when Magnus left.

As the cab approaches the red light by the square the music and the now slower and—so it seems—louder vibrations caused by the cobblestones have a curious effect on my mind. *This ride is rather a rough one for a magic carpet*, I muse as I softly apply my foot to the brake bringing the vehicle to a full stop and at the same time silencing the engine. A brief intermission follows during which the wind and string sections of the Czech Philharmonic build up towards a melodious release. But the hopeful rise suddenly crumbles and disintegrates into a series of darker, feebler and more fragmented attempts at a beauty recreated. And as though the spheres have been listening, a huge black cloud at that moment erases the face of the moon from the skies.

Because I never know where to look for the next customer, I experience a pang of indecision. For an instant I don't know which way to turn. As it is, I never make up my mind. I only find out where I am going when the light turns green and with my foot on the speeder I wake the engine. Slowly, almost soundlessly, the cab cruises across the canal-bridge in the direction of the city center. But why does it bother me not to have decided on the direction I am going? Since the next customer can be anywhere and at this time of the evening is hard to come by, it really does not matter one way or the other. Why then the discomfort? Is it because I lack faith? I don't think so. On the contrary, I believe that as long as I do something, keep on doing it, and go somewhere I will eventually get to where I need to be. All roads lead to Rome is what I have been told. Nevertheless I have never been able to rid myself of the feeling that there is a wrong way, that it might be the one I have taken, and that it is by now too late to turn around.

With the engine softly purring the cab glides across Knippels Bridge connecting the islands Amager and Zealand. On the left appears the tarnished and forbidding old stock exchange with the dragon tower and on the right the heavy black steel and glass silhouette of the National Bank. The sky is dark and heavy and out of it falls a few drops. Not yet the promised torrent, and not enough even to start the windshield wipers. However, it is enough to reflect the city lights and blur the visibility slightly. The bells and drums and wind instruments prepare the announcement of the final and most melodious part of the first movement. The strings in chorus rise higher and higher until something snaps and there is a silence that would have been unbearable if it had not been broken by flutes. Still no customers and now I am already by the lakes on the perimeter of the center. What the hell? So, the sky is pitch black and soggy as a wet sponge. But there is no deluge. After all this is so pleasant: To be sitting comfortably with my forebodings in a warm taxi filled with Mahler's Ninth Symphony; to be watching the shiny lakes float by to the sound of dark and somber harpstrings; to disengage from the general big city static, the far-off sirens of a patrolcar; to be on the lookout and one moment finding myself by the sea in a newly built part of town, only the next to be squeezing through the twisted streets of the old city. One moment to be alone with my thoughts and the next to find myself in conversation with a total stranger. Softly encased, as in a womb on wheels, conjuring spontaneity. Obeying impulses. Letting go. In all kinds of weather, through all four seasons of the year. Cognizant of the changes that the city undergoes, from when the shift begins during rush-hour, from crowded sidewalks and bicycle lanes, until the streets are deserted at midnight. Neon-signs reflected in parked cars and lakes and puddles; wet blur of advertisements and street-lights mirroring in pavements; elegant hotel facades with their prism-candelabras; windswept emptinesses of abandoned parking lots; warm glow from restaurants and serving houses; wooden skiffs and fishing boats rubbing sides in harbors and canals; royal monuments and sumptuous residential palaces in one end of the city contrasting with the Nigerian prostitutes saying "hi darling" to their potential customers on a god-forsaken street corner of another. The human squalor congregated outside the welfare shelter in the early evening, drug deals, deranged drunk shouting, guy flashing his butt and pissing, pants down on his feet by the Pillar of Freedom. All of it statements of sorts, messages… To me the taxi driver?

Perhaps, but if so, none of it detracts from the pleasure I experience cruising the night in my cab. Even if the purpose is to make money, I have made up my mind never to let this purpose get in the way of my enjoyment. Regaling my senses I take in the fantastic shapes of the roof-tops and chimney-pots silhouetted against the luminous summer sky or the heavy black sky of winter. Those forever transforming skies of Copenhagen. The moods of both the city and the man observing it, listening to the first movement of Mahler's Ninth Symphony, anticipating the second. Ever so slowly I cruise the night streets of my native city with one finger on the steering wheel and one eye on the world around me.

2.

Imagining the quick waltz that is to initiate the second movement, I once again find myself by the lakes. I try to keep my eyes on the street but they keep straying to the lit facades on the other side and the colorful reflections of neon-advertisements on the black surface of the water.

The central sends me to pick up an elderly Swedish lady on crutches. She speaks nostalgically about shovelling snow in freezing Freetown Christiania in 1978, eating hot chicken broth in a lesbian commune and dancing "Afro" at night in a frozen childrens' meadow.

I drop her off at the main train station and head for the music hall Vega where a concert has just ended. Throngs of people are pouring out of the place. Any time now someone will climb into my cab and ask to be taken somewhere. Waiting for it to happen I become aware of the weight in my jacket of the soft, old, red wallet from Israel that has been my taxi-companion from the very beginning, forty years ago. I wonder that after all those years, after everything I have been through, I again find myself in a cab, waiting for a customer to separate from the crowd and enter my space. People are hugging each other and mounting bikes all around me. Taking it all in and feeling the weight of change in my inside pocket, I think of fate. It was the same day my Israeli actor and taxi-driver friend suggested going back to taxi driving for a third period that I came across the old Israeli wallet in my desk drawer. This apparent coincidence became like a sign to me. Was driving a taxi the occupation that the Fates had in mind for me all along?

How did it come about that I started to drive a taxi those forty years ago? From where did I get the idea? If someone inspired me, I no longer remember. When I first acquired the license to drive a taxi, I was a twenty-two-year old student of history at the University of Copenhagen who needed money for rent, food, concert-tickets and beer. During this, my first period as a taxi driver, it had not yet occurred to me that one day I would write novels and essays. Having spent my seventeenth year as a high-school exchange student in Palo Alto California, I saw myself in a future job as correspondent for Denmark's Radio in Washington D.C. It was with this objective in mind that I wrote term papers on subjects like "The American Revolution" and "The New Deal."

No, plan A did most certainly not include the taxi. And neither did, for that matter, any plan B or C. Where I grew up such a thing was off limits. I come from a family of means. My parents were highly educated and cultured people, who lived the life of upper middle class Denmark. To them it was simply unthinkable that a child of theirs would want to make a living as a taxi driver. Not that I always did what my parents expected me to. Far from it. But still I was a product of their social environment. If I had announced my intention of becoming a taxi driver, which I might well have done, my father would have laughed at what he recognized as a provocation. And he would have been right. If I rebelled against my surroundings (they seemed to always know better than me what I had to do) it was not from any lack of ambition. I, too, wanted to do some particular thing and do it well. Only, I wanted to decide what it was for myself and do it in a way native to my character.

However, during the years when I was a student at the University of Copenhagen, taxi driving was not only an acceptable but also an independent way of making money. I could have a car more or less whenever I wanted one and never had to drive when I did not want to. I could take a break and have dinner with my wife. I could go on driving until dawn or stop at midnight. It was all up to me. Married, but as yet with no children to provide for, it was no big deal earning whatever it took to pay for a new record player, a trip to Greece, a ticket to a concert with Joni Mitchell or a night on the town. Compared to now when I have teenage kids and am in my third and, as it were, terminal period of taxi driving, during the first period there was no pressure. Even if the salary was as lousy in those years (1976-80) as it is today, it was more lucrative. Since Danish law did not yet require taxis to have sensors in the seats, the vehicle did not know if there were customers in it. Neither did the owner or the tax-authorities. A customer would hail the cab and negotiate a price that suited the two involved parties and did not directly involve any absent ones. In those days, making good money in a cab was so easy that not only was I able to wine and dine my wife, but I was also able to buy us a little car to drive around in.

Money, however, was not enough to save the marriage. But even so my cab driving continued after my divorce. It continued after I lost interest in becoming a correspondent. It continued after I abandoned my empty flat, still full of the things my wife had left behind when she bailed. Most importantly it continued even after I decided to cut the rope tying me to my old life. That is, it continued when in 1978 I moved into the Freetown of Christiania to squat in a small wooden wagon and set to work on becoming a novelist.

During my three-year spell in Christiania I did not drive a taxi frequently. (I had very little need of money and very much need of time to write). I drove a little and kept doing it until I left for France. After

41

living from hand to mouth for a year and a half in Paris, I was flown to California by the woman I was in love with. By the time I came back to my native city three years later, still unpublished and with no education, no money, no love of my life, no wagon and no prospects, it did not occur to me to drive a taxi. Instead I set to work on a novel with a vehemence I had never before experienced. As a matter of fact it is doubtful that I would ever have taken up taxi driving again, had I not (three years later when I was finishing the revision of my novel) been prodded by my friend, the bald pianist Knulp, who was in the process of getting his taxi license and proposed that if we drove on the same nights, we could round off with a beer.

Thus started the second period of my taxi driving. That was in November 1987. Since I had last worked as a taxi driver, smoking had been banned and—non-electronic—credit cards had been introduced. Many customers paid the precise amount and never mentioned a tip. Also there were now sensors in all the seats. As a result I had to drive longer hours in order to make less money than before. Still, I continued until 1992, when I needed to get out of Denmark and got on a train to Prague. It was shortly after the Velvet Revolution in my father's native Czechoslovakia (my mother was a Dane) that set the individual Czech and Slovak free and made it possible for foreigners to settle in the country. If things worked out, I was going to stay in Prague and never return to Denmark. Of course this time nothing was further from my mind than driving a cab. In fact it was as perfectly absent as if I had never had anything to do with it.

Little did I know, however, that patient fate had not lost sight of its design for me and was just waiting for the right moment to complete the circle. Whether I liked it or not the taxicab was to come back for the third period that started a little over two years ago, in November 2014.

3.

Three horn blasts followed by three from the string section introduce the rondo burlesque, which Mahler wanted to be very defiant. And at that moment the door to the passenger seat opens. A woman looks in and asks me if I am free. I think of the Free sign glowing green on my roof. I nod: "Yes ma'am. Sure am." She says "good" and gets in. When she tells me the name of the street she wants to go to, I hand her my stock line about how I only recently took up taxi driving again after twenty-two years and did not know the place.

In point of fact this piece of information is somewhat of a misrepresentation, considering that I am now over two years into my third period. In the beginning it was meant simply as an excuse for not knowing the destination. But as I grew more and more streetwise and began to understand the means I had at my disposal my motive gradually changed; nowadays I very often give my stock line even if I know perfectly well the street the customer is going to. Why? Because more than I am the taxi driver I appear to be in the eyes of a stranger, I am a taxidriving writer in a bind who tries to survive by driving. In other words, I set this, my third period, apart from both the first and the second. The difference is that I am not any more a man without a reputation in the public mind. I have written and published nine books. Some with Danish or Czech publishers. And some self-published. The fact that I cannot count on the Danish media and am unable any more to publish with the official Danish press (since I left the country for Prague) and being almost never invited to give public readings, have turned the taxicab into my main vehicle for establishing contact with readers who either know my books, keep one or more of them at home, have heard of them or would possibly like to read them if only they knew of their existence. My stock line is my way of encouraging people to ask what I have been doing these last twenty-two years.

Roughly there are four reactions: The one I aim for is the customer asking me what I have been doing all that time. But sometimes it is perceived as an invitation to talk about the changes in the cab, the city and society in general of the last quarter century. The third reaction is no reaction at all; the customer reaches for his smartphone and starts scrolling. The fourth (and most interesting to me as a novelist) is the one this single, forty-eight-year old, concert-going woman sitting next to me on this evening offered: her own story!

43

Twenty-two years ago, she was four years into the marriage to the father of her children; he had left her only a month before to be with a twenty-eight-year old. He was and he remained her wonderful husband. "It is downright terrifying," she says, "how this young woman has turned his head." She has now made him so confused that he firmly believes he loves her. As the woman is telling me this, she is staring out through the windshield and shaking her head hopelessly. Their grown kids refuse to see him. They think it is not so much his heart he has lost as his mind. Now the house has to be sold, and she is seeing a psychologist. But, she says with an ironic smile, even if she is shellshocked, she is still going to concerts alone. Smiling now, she turns to me: "Because life must go on, right! It was a good concert, sure, but…" As she stops a tear drops to her cheek. How could he do it? He was such a wonderful husband for twenty-six years. As if all this time did not mean a thing. But it did. They had travelled places and been very happy together…

Stopped outside the house that has a "for sale" sign up, I try to comfort the woman by piling a bunch of cliches on her head: I tell her that worrying never did anybody any good. Things are what they are and will be what they will be. It is a tough time she is going through, but she must trust in the restorative forces at work in the soul. Time will heal her wounds and she will move on. Very likely she will one day look back and realize that the suffering served a purpose.

She has pressed her pin-code on the pay-terminal, dried her tears in her handkerchief, thanked me for lending her my ear, gotten out and unlocked the empty house, when immediately after the name Jespersen and an address pop up on the monitor. With a flick of the finger I confirm. Crumpling the receipt that the woman did not want, I am already on my way.

Turns out Jespersen is an architect in his late forties, headed for the city to have a few drinks with a Frenchman whom he calls his "French connection." When I have given him my stock line, he immediately falls into the first category and asks what I have been doing for twenty-two years. I tell him I have written and published six novels, three books of essays and a lot of articles in the newspapers. Jespersen's eyes are open wide when he asks my name. And when I give it to him he is flabbergasted.

"I'll be damned," he says and bends forward in the back seat. So… that means he is sitting in a cab driven by the author of *Victim of Welfare. An Essay on State and Individual in Denmark*! And when I confirm, Jespersen announces his wish to keep driving around a bit longer in order for us to talk about the book. That is… if I don't mind? To hell with the price, and the Frenchman can wait ten minutes. Not long ago, Jespersen has reread the essay and there is so much we must discuss. But first I must tell him why I drive a taxi? Is it because it is a way of meeting people, or is it because I need the money? What is the lowdown on it all?

Since he has read the essay twice, I say, he will know how I lived around and from hand to mouth as I worked on a novel. He will also know how I was interrogated by the tax-authorities and finally fined for not having had any contact with the State. He knows all that. The only thing he does not know is what the consequences were of publishing the essay. At first the book created a tremendous stir. Newpapers sent interviewers to Prague; I was in all the Danish media as a sort of modern tax Robin Hood; an excerpt from the essay was distributed to the members of the parliamentary subcommission on taxation; finally the minister of taxation had to answer publicly to "the case of the exiled author Per Smidl." And all the while my second novel *Chop Suey* was selling well. If my future had not been made before (when *Chop Suey* was on the bestseller list) it surely was now. Or so I thought. But I could not have been more mistaken. When the storm eased and the waves died down something like an ominous quiet followed. And when the publisher who had published *Chop Suey* wrote me to say that they wanted to annul the contract for my third novel *Mathias Kraft* (it had already been submitted and accepted) I knew I was in trouble.

"But, hey," I say to Jespersen, "this ride is getting rather expensive. Now you know what happened and why you met me in this cab. Gotta make some money. And besides I also have two teenage kids to feed!"

In the end Jespersen pays me a hundred kroner cash tip on top of the by then tripled fare. He assures me he is going to make all his friends buy the essay so that in the future I need not drive a taxi any more. It is really and truly a shame, he says as he prepares to exit in front of the expensive bar on The Kings New Square, that the "rotten individuals" who only wreak damage on life wallow in money, while people, authors and artists, have to drive taxis in order to just barely scrape through. And as if in affirmation of this statement, he nods one final time before getting out. Speaking through the open door he repeats his offer to pay my drinks if I will call it a night and join him and the French connection. And when I—again—shake my head, he closes the door leaving me to my fate. Alone again I get out my little notebook and jot down "Jespersen architect." Replacing it to my shirt pocket and leaving the curb, I feel somewhat gratified that even if at sixty I have had to take up the cab again for the third time in forty years, and even if my work as a writer has cost me my livelihood, it is paying off in other if more roundabout ways.

4.

A sea of strings softly swelling announces the next to last adagio that Mahler composed before he died. I am cruising slowly along my standard route in "District 215" (behind the main trainstation) where there are people out 24/7 and a possibility of being waved down. The monitor shows that I am number three in line if a customer calls my company for a cab. When it is my turn, a sound sort of like a mechanical turkey will announce the advent of an address on the screen. It can happen two minutes from now or it can happen in half an hour. As far as turnover is concerned the evening has been lousy. Even for dead January when everybody and everything is wasted after Christmas consumption and New Year's. Trying not to worry about the money I need and am not making, I dream of the rich tourist waiting for me around the next corner and wanting a tour of the city. Somehow or another I usually manage to convince myself that things will work out in the end. I call my doubtful heart to order by telling *myself* that nothing good ever came from worrying, and that it is useless to fret just because the going is a bit hard. And right there and then as I am admonishing myself about these things, I remember the woman who had been abandoned by her husband. When I told her all this stuff about things going to work out all right in the end, I was in earnest. I believed it myself. Telling myself the same right now, I am not so sure. Despite Jespersen, money is definitely not pouring in, and an empty feeling grows in me as I keep driving around the same streets. One more futile round and I will match the old record of eight such rounds from last January. Nine and I will have set a new one. Where Gustav Mahler left his Ninth Symphony to posterity, I Per Smidl taxi driver in Copenhagen will at least have left this testimony to a ninth and record-breaking round in search of a customer. A small personal triumph of sorts. But… if that is how it must be, well, then so be it.

Suddenly it strikes me that the symphonic experience is one more way the taxicab employs to fit me out with the street wisdom a man needs in order to cope with emptiness. Indeed in order to live and survive. What it wants me to learn is not just the names of the streets but also where to find them, what they lead to if one goes down them, and why it is necessary to do so if one is to know. In other words the cab teaches me the *meaning of choice and direction.* On the superficial level it is true that since I took up driving a taxi again two years ago, Copenhagen has endeavored to present itself to me merely as a sum total of streets, thoroughfares, markets, restaurants, hotels, squares, monuments, cinemas, theatres, brothels, cafes, concert halls, sports arenas, dormitories, educational and correctional facilities, museums, art-galleries, hospitals, swinger clubs, cocktail bars, discotheques, churches, gas-stations, company headquarters, music venues, schools, shopping centers and metro-stations. On the deeper level, however, all the customers' destinations put together seem to indicate that there may be just one end to be found but various ways of reaching it.

Starting out in the last daylight, right on the edge of dusk, I cruise these winter streets until after midnight. Rolling with the ebb and flowing with the tide I register the erratic and uneven pulse of the city and observe the subtle stages it goes through; from the workaday population of seemingly sober individuals hurriedly going about their business to the drunks, homeless, criminals and prostitutes of the night; from the stressful rush-hour to a sort of repose or exhaustion in sleep's oblivion.

Outside the men's welfare shelter and emerging from a motley assortment of human misery, a scarecrow of a man hails me from the curb. Believing that eye contact with the customer is important, I twist myself around to look at him as he gets in the back seat. And while the adagio screeches its way towards the final gasp, the guy with a strangely doughy and sunken face counts the coins in his hand. "Is fifty-nine enough to go to...," he gives me a destination that would cost at least two hundred and fifty kroner to reach. I tell him that he is over two hundred short, but that he is welcome to stay and get warm a few minutes. And it is while we are sitting there, listening to Mahler preparing for the end, that through the windshield I spot a prostitute I remember picking up at her basement place lit by a red bulb about a month ago. I even remember that her name is Kiki and that she is originally from Laos. She is on her way into the same sex shop that she asked me to stop in front of the night I drove her. She had to get some viagra for the customer, who was waiting for her in the hotel I was taking her to. I took a mental note of the place in case I should ever be in acute need of a helping hand from chemistry myself; and it was right after she came back with the viagra that she asked me if my cock was "small, medium, large or perhaps... medium-large?" When I replied "medium to medium large I guess," she just said "Huh," like my answer was a disappointment to her. In any case she proceeded to inform me that Danish men were the best lovers in the world and that she ought to know, because she had tried all nationalities. The forty-year-old Jutlander she was going to see, would ride her all night until morning. She loved very much to screw, she confided. Did I, too?

"I sure do!" I said.

"Then get yourself a little bit of this..." she waved the bag with the blue pills at me, "and... come see me sometime. Here's my business card!"

Still sitting there with the junkie in the back seat, I come to think of other customers that taught me something. Like the French brain scientist from Lille who told me of the importance of sleep. "A good night's sleep is like a brand new dishwasher," he said. During the day we filled the machine with our dirty dishes, and during the night it washed them for us. And now, as I am asking the junkie to leave, I am thinking of other guys like him who were not only able to pay the fare, but also insisted on tipping me their last penny; this in stark contrast to the successful graphic designer, the real estate broker, the corporate lawyer, the investment banker, the politician or the insurance CEO. As opposed to the bums, barflies and criminals I sometimes get in my cab, these stuffed shirts with large electronic bank accounts just give their pin-codes to the pay terminal and leave without so much as a word.

There really seems no end to the teachings of the taxicab. From the banal to the profound; from the prejudices confirmed or eliminated as the case might be. Like that memorable evening last early spring when the monitor's mechanical turkey sound sent me to an address in my district. As I drive up, the door to the building is opened and a no longer young woman appears wearing an atrocious blond wig and strutting a pair of positively terrifying tits. Phony from top to toe in her stilettos she sort of advances to where I am standing by the cab, waiting. Like some evil omen from a future full of cyborgs, she steps up close to me and says: "I'm going to the reality TV-awards in the Circus Building and..." Here she bats her outrageous eyelashes at me in such a way I fear they will fall off. "I am nominated for the best tits in town!" Breathing her perfume and involuntarily glancing at the protruding nominees, I feel cold shivers down my spine.

If ever there was a prejudice confirmed, this was it. This plastic surgery product with a nose ridge sharper than a razor's edge perfectly matched the picture I had formed in my mind of what such reality-TV people were like.

But what do you know? Later that same evening as I am cruising by the Circus Building, I am hailed by the most celebrated of Danish boob jobs. The sister of a former Formel 1 racing champ, this woman's remarkable fame is built on a pair of tits not a bit less terrifying in their ridiculous proportions than the nominated ones. I had of course heard of her before. From the gossip magazines I had read in waiting rooms here and there, I knew the surgical history of her boobs. But this was the first time I ever met her in the flesh as it were. My heart skips a beat as she gets into the passenger seat of my cab. Next thing I know, she looks sort of defiantly at me and announces that she must sit on the safety belt with her butt. She has a doctor's notice to the effect that it could jeopardize the "health and shape" of her breasts, if she wore the belt on her chest and I slammed the brakes. What I want to say is "Heaven forbid." But instead I assure her that as long as it is all right with the car—it makes a terrible racket if a seatbelt is not fastened—this is no problem with me. Then as politely as I can, I ask her to raise her butt just a wee bit, so I can pull the seat belt under her. She giggles, and as she bends forward as far as the boobs permit and raises her butt at the same time, she flashes me a naughty smile. Resolutely I pull the belt under her and stick it in the slot. "All right, we're off," I say as I put the car in gear.

Driving along with the celebrity next to me, I am wondering what it would be like for a man to have intercourse with a pair of artificial tits of that size. Would they stand straight up in the air or implode softly to a sunny-side up, like natural ones, when she is on her back? Or would she perhaps pull out from between them a doctor's notice exempting her also from the missionary position? And if that happened, then what? How, indeed, would a man cope? To embrace her, a man would need arms at least the length of an orangutan's. I wanted to ask her these things and if her bras were tailor made, but deciding that I was after all just a cab driver and all of this really besides the point and none of my business, I held my tongue. Instead I struck up a conversation by asking her, if she was comfortable sitting on the safety belt. At this she again smiled warmly at me and nodded her head; and as though she had read my thoughts and also with a pinch of amusement in her voice, she said it was gentlemanly of me to ask, but I should not think of her as some fragile article to be handled with care. People always thought she was more bust than brain, but as a scorpio, robust was really more like it.

She said this with such self irony, I could not help laughing. And suddenly I felt relieved. Chockful of prejudices against this queen of the reality-tv world as I had been before, I was surprised to find that I actually *liked* her. The remarkable thing was that despite the phony tits and glistening lips, she came off as a real human being. On top of that she had made me laugh! And I think she must have liked me a little bit too, because in an apparent need to confide in someone, she now told me how it was a major disappointment to her, that this year she had not been nominated "best tits in town." "Oh no!" I exclaimed out of commiseration. Out of the corner of my eye I glanced at the scorned ones. Even if I liked her I could not for the life of me fathom what made a woman (who was from her maker fitted out with well-shaped, proportional and soft breasts) have such artificial monsters made instead. Notwithstanding, I thought she deserved an award for coming across to a stranger like me as a warm human being *in spite of* them. But, alas, there was and never will be a category for this sort of thing.

After the celebrity star had left me (with a finger kiss), I got out the little green notebook that I always carry in my shirt posket. In it I wrote the time and the place I had picked her up, how she had a doctor's notice, how she made me laugh and said farewell with a finger kiss. At the end I wrote: what does it matter if a woman has artificial tits if only her soul is naturally beautiful. The tits may be in the way, but the soul is what counts.

Sitting there with the notebook open, my eyes fall on the name Willy the Weasel and my thoughts begin to wander. I recall how I did not know whether to stop for him or not. With his tatooed neck, mohican hair and clean shaven face, he looked for all the world like someone out on parole after serving twenty years for homicide. Approaching the place he was standing, he seemed positively scary to me. Yet, being on my fourth or fifth round along the standard streets, next thing I know I had stopped for him. He had gotten in the passenger seat, had given me an address a half hour drive away, and I had given him my stock line. I should not worry, he told me. He knew where he was living. He would help. Twenty-two years was a long time, he mused. When I stopped driving the taxi, his girlfriend was only eight-years-old. Tomorrow was her thirtieth birthday. They were going to go out to a restaurant they liked. Just the two of them. Nothing fancy. She was "very" pregnant and had to be cautious. They both did. Theirs was a long story. Willy gave me his hand and said his name was Willy. Willy the Weasel. The nickname he got when in prison he bit the little finger off one of the other inmates.

After we were done shaking hands, Willy shook his head in wonder. It was hard to believe, he said, that his girlfriend was now pregnant. She had been a lot of things in her life, but pregnant was—or so he thought—not one of them. The night he met her on the railroad bridge eleven years ago, she was nineteen, addicted to heroin and working the streets to get her stuff. And in addition to this "fucked up CV" she was also sick with the hepatitis she had contracted from a used syringe. It had taken them over seven years and his two prison sentences for "turning pimps into pulp" to

51

get her a better CV. And just as things had looked like they might succeed, he was jailed… again. Two more years! But rain or shine she came to see him every single time she was allowed. She was there for him in his time of need just like he had been there for her, when she was ill and on junk and a pain in the ass. She could never understand why he had done "all that" for her. No matter what he did or said, she didn't believe he really loved her. But he did and that is why he stood by her. Why he pulped the pimps and always took her back and forgave her the shit she pulled. And look at her now! She was so beautiful one would not think it was the same woman. He had been out almost two years, and she was pregnant. The two of them were going out to a restaurant. They were going to have a child together. After all they had been through. Who would ever have thought it possible!

"Are you a father?" Willy turned his head and looked me in the eye.

I nodded: "I have two kids. A boy and a girl. The boy is the oldest."

Willy said that for him it was hard to believe. It was like it was almost too good to be true. That he—*he* with *his* CV—was to become something he, himself, had never known: a father! And even if he tried to shake the thought, he could not help wondering if they would make it with all the shit they carried around in their luggage. But… maybe. His girlfriend had been free of heroin for years, and now she was also finally free of the disease. He was able to provide for them both, nay… the three of them. The evil cloud seemed to have lifted. So, yes… maybe. Maybe together they could give their child a better beginning than they had had themselves. "A good beginning is all!" Willy said as he handed me the banknote and told me to keep the rest. He opened the door to leave.

Seconds later, his dark figure disappeared between the drab building blocks leaving no other trace behind than seven short lines in my notebook and the memory of a man, violent when a pimp hurt his loved one, but otherwise gentle, softspoken, kind and generous.

•

That night on my way back to my usual haunts, I was thinking of the magic that the cab works on some people. I wondered what it was about the cab that made total strangers confide so readily in each other? First, I remember thinking it had to do with the small and warm intimacy of the taxicab's interior. Second, I thought it due to the late hour and the drinks that usually had been consumed prior to our encounter. Third, the magic created probably owed to the accidental nature of the situation, the feeling that our company was only a fleeting moment, and we were never going to see each other again. Last and by no means least, I thought it had to do with the more or less permanent need to lighten our burden combined with the seeming inability of doing so with the ones closest to us—either for fear of hurting others' feelings or of laying our souls bare for their eyes to see and their bitterness to take advantage of.

Later on this taxi night in dead January, as Mahler's Ninth Symphony draws to its end in a series of soft, as if prolonged and ever thinner strings of light and darkness, I again find myself pondering the teachings of my taxicab. The road that has brought me back to it has hardly been without its share of disaster and suffering. And yet this, the brief human encounters, is my reward. Without my ever asking for it, and as if it were unpremeditated, the job as cab driver during the last two years has taken me into every corner of the city I once left and tried to forget about. Without my planning it or wanting it or even thinking about it, the cab has arranged for me to meet the individual men and women who together make up the population. Teaching me... what? To write or how to be a better writer? Hardly, but maybe the lesson that in living as in writing (and driving a cab) it pays off speaking to a person's heart straight away without any other ulterior motive than dragging the truth out in the open.

Besides getting in the way of judging my fellow human beings on the basis of their breast-size, dress, hairdo or tattoos, in short my own ingrown prejudices, the cab keeps impressing on me the truth that no matter what else people may be in terms of social position, religious and sexual orientation, skin color, there is always infinitely more to them than meets the eye. The falling out between me and the Danish state, my fall from grace and the necessity to provide for my teenage children, all of which together drove me back into the taxicab! My permanent need for more money than I am able to earn! Considering all this, is it any wonder that today as I write this, the cab stands out as the incarnation of my personal success, failure and eventual survival—like some invisible price-tag, forever attached to non-conformity.

While driving a cab might not be what I wanted to do in life, it is undeniably what I have ended up doing. As such it is not to be put aside as of inferior value or less importance. It is paramount to my well-being that I keep acknowledging this in order to defend myself against not only bitterness and paranoia, but also to experience the joy of being which is, after all, the purpose of our existence. It is paramount that I learn to live, not what I wanted to happen and planned for, but what actually and in reality happened. What is happening: the meaning of an outcast cruising the city in a taxicab and being taught the lesson of acceptance.

All right! So, I was not supposed ever again to have to drive a cab for a living. In Prague I lived predominantly from my writings in Czech and Danish and did not consider returning to Denmark. But then, even if a return was not on my agenda, it was what happened. If only I could read the stars, I am sure they would tell me that in spite of all my youthful plans, this cab—and nothing else—is what I was destined for. This very situation that I am living and, for so long found to be unjust, is my lot. Believing this to be true, today I not only accept the sequence of events and my place indiscriminately, but also embrace it all and enjoy it. The first few weeks I drove the cab after the long break, I grumbled that I had to learn the use of a GPS and relearn the map of Copenhagen. Not so anymore. Even if today it takes time away from my writing, I have grown to love the feeling of magnificent solitude as I cruise through the Copenhagen streets never knowing who or what awaits around the next corner. Sleet, hail, pouring rain, mist or sunshine—every moment of the way I am thankful to be me all alone and knowing it to be right and as it should be. Whether or not I once dreamt of literary prizes and official recognition, whether or not I had other plans, got out of line and messed things up is not of any import. This cab is what happened and what is happening. It is my life, my time, my place and portion. It is what is (left of) me in the company of my contemporaries.

Tonight as Mahler's Ninth Symphony goes into its terminal throes of departure, I think that should it so happen that I cannot publish any more novels, I can at least drive this night-cab, dream of the (unwritten) books that my life and the customers' confessions inspire and rejoice that I am—after all—still alive.

TRADING SECRETS AT THE MELANCHOLY HOUSE

Jayne Thompson

Recently at a juvenile detention center, a young man, Corey, called me over to his table. Corey wasn't doing any of the writing activities I had planned for the day. Instead, he read from his copy of *Letters to My Younger Self: An Anthology of Writings by Incarcerated Men at S.C.I. Graterford and a Writing Workbook*. I didn't blame him. The administration had told me that the copies of *Letters* and the notebooks I had brought with me would be taken up at the end of the session and would be available to the young people upon their release. In other words, what few words they could read during our hour and a half session would be all they could read of it until they left for home or another facility. "They might fashion a weapon out of the book," the administrator said and closed the discussion.

The men in my Graterford Prison class had written the book for these young people; I think the men had envisioned the children lying on their cots in their cells at night reading the book and taking the men's wisdom to heart. At least I know that is what I imagined. I have given a copy of the book to hundreds of children in detention centers, but this was the first time I had heard that they couldn't keep it with them in their cells. I wondered if this was always the case.

Corey asked me, "Why would these men at Graterford write this for us? For no pay. They don't even have their full names in it. I don't get it."

I replied, "They care about you. They don't want to meet you at Gra-

terford. They want this to be the last of your days spent incarcerated."
Corey was reading D. Saadiq P.'s "Deep Blue Sea." I added, "Saadiq wrote
that after class one night when he was worried that his son was going
down a path that would land him in prison. I love this piece, especially
how he ends it."

"Yeah." Corey nodded and bent his head to the book. In a voice on
the precipice of gravely manhood, he read aloud from the poem's ending:

> Naw, son, this is the Black sea,
> the deep dark place where
> you don't wanna be.
> Where everyone looks and feels like me
> full of pain and despair in this
> sea of stale air.
> Take heed to my words or this
> will be your destiny, because the
> road you're heading down
> has already got the best of me.
>
> So I hope you see what I didn't see
> and follow the Blue sea
> and not the Black sea that has
> swallowed me.

I understand Corey's bewilderment. I had asked grown men who
live with a gigantic amount of regret every day if they would look very
deeply into themselves and tell a story of a time when they had done
something between the ages of 11-17 that still sits uncomfortably in
their conscience—or to tell of an event that occurred in their youth
that led them to future mistakes. They also wrote of historical and
societal scars. When I look at it now, I can see that the entire project
was filled with pain. The Graterford guys never once complained
or balked at an assignment. Instead, they were excited to create the
book, to have a chance to speak to the young people they longed to
help guide. So often they expressed their frustration at not being

able to advise new generations of young people, their sons, daughters, young people they saw in the news, and imagined strangers. Prison has walled the men off from communication. Writing put a small hole in the wall.

I would like to tell you that I did not know of the pain I was asking the men to endure by writing these stories and poems. After many classes, I drove down the long dark driveway and worried about what I was doing. If I didn't believe, didn't know from first-hand experience, that writing heals, I would not ask them to write of such painful experiences, I assured myself. But I am not a therapist, and I did not know what to tell them about the scars they were left to probe alone in the darkness of their cells.

> *Let the doors be of iron; and let the grating occasioned by opening and shutting them extend a sound that shall deeply pierce the soul.—Benjamin Rush, physician, founding father and founding member of the Philadelphia Society for Alleviating the Miseries of Public Prisons, 1787*

One night during the early stages of writing *Letters*, twenty men and I sat in a circle in the prison classroom, me, in the seat of honor, a metal chair with hunter green upholstery now torn after years of use instead of high school hard chairs with attached desks that the bigger men like Chris squeezed themselves into. The night's reading led us to discussing the brain's resistance to prodding when we are attempting to write. Some of the men explained that they were having trouble writing—they didn't remember much—and they wondered if their forgetting was a defense mechanism. Others expressed that their childhood held more sadness than happiness—or that is the way it seemed to them when they began to write.

Paul volunteered to read a draft of a letter he had written to his mother who died when he was five:

> I wish I had an image of you in my mind, but most of my memory of you is just feeling, an emotion. I can't believe it's been nearly five decades since you left. I needed to write

this letter to tell you that, in all those years, you never left my heart. I often wish I could travel back in time to when I was that sensitive little boy who loved to fall asleep sitting on your lap while hugging you with my head resting on the cushion of your breast.

I never blamed you for leaving. No one who witnessed the years of brutal beatings you suffered at Daddy's hands could blame you. Sometimes I wonder if the hate and anger that boiled inside me throughout my youth was more about your leaving than what he did to you. Maybe it was just camouflage to hide the guilt and shame of loving a father who tortured and tormented the person I loved more than anyone or anything in the world. In my mind, your death was not just a suicide; it was also a murder, and Daddy was the killer.

I saw you leap out of your bedroom window that night. I think something important inside me shattered when you crashed through the glass. That window symbolized the best part of my life, broken into a thousand pieces scattered around your twisted body lying on the cold concrete in front of our house on Oriana Street. I didn't know at the time that I would eventually become a predator roaming the streets of that very same neighborhood. Didn't know that Daddy's dark heart would infect me like a contagious disease, that his rage and violence would become mine.

The class clapped and made appreciative comments and gestures, giving me time to consider what I could say after hearing that story, time to swallow and try to recover my voice. My mind rushed, my thoughts collided. I said, "God…"

Every year the Lifer's Association hosts a banquet. In my seven years as a teacher for the Prison Literacy Project, I have gone to quite a few of these lunches. Lifers, their families and friends, and invited teachers and prison volunteers gather for lunch in the gymnasium for what the men tell me is the best food of the year. Soon after Paul's reading of his letter, I sat at a banquet table with Paul and his two brothers, one older, one younger, all tall, broad-shouldered men, like their father had been.

"Tell me what Paul was like as a boy," I asked.

"He was angry," his younger brother said. "One time he walked up to a little boy and took his ice cream money right out of his hand. We didn't have money for extras."

The older brother added, "I took the money from Paul and gave it back to the boy. He would do things like that, but he was a good kid." He laughed.

Paul interrupted, "Remember that time we were all in the station wagon going on a picnic, Daddy, Mommy, and us three."

Paul's older brother said, "That wasn't Mommy."

Paul answered, "It was, too, Mommy." The older brother reached across the table and touched Paul's hand, "That was the woman who came after Mommy died." The stories stopped.

Perhaps the line in Cormac McCarthy's *The Road* is correct: "You forget what you want to remember and you remember what you want to forget."

Back in class, I told my Graterford guys of a visit I had made all alone to Eastern State Penitentiary one cold clear day in December. In 1929, incarcerated men at Eastern State built Graterford, a fact that disturbs me every time I enter the series of steel doors leading to our classroom. I was working on a difficult piece of autobiographical writing at the time and looking to escape my brain, but what drew me to Eastern was something deeper than that. The radial hub, the spokes, the separate, locked cells—I recognized Eastern as the resistant mind's twin, and I drew my coat close. With the audio tour headphones on, I stood that day in the prison's hub, turning slowly round and round, surveilling the quiet corridors that spread out like wheel spokes, I realized that the brain faces more than resistance—the brain sometimes locks its memories in separate cells, and there is no master key.

In the 1820s, Quaker reformers believed that solitary confinement at Eastern State Penitentiary, or Cherry Hill as it was known in its early days for the cherry orchard that once stood on the spot, would offer the inmates a way to the "inner light"—an awareness of the divine spark present in all people. That awareness would lead to repentance. The reformers forbade prisoner-to-prisoner conversations; the prisoners' days should be spent in quiet contemplation of their crimes. Guards wore socks over their shoes to soften the sound of heels on the floor and placed hoods over the prisoners' heads for the few times they took a prisoner out of his or her cell. Prisoners received light from the "eye of God," a skylight above their cells, which allowed them to read the Bible and inspirational materials, the only texts allowed in the early days. After the appointed time of reflection, inmates worked at jobs such as cobbler or weaver. Heating and ventilation proved a challenge, but the heating system was top-of-the-line in its time; pipes filled with hot water moved through, taking a bit of the chill off the cell. The pipes also ran though the corridor so that guards could hear if prisoners tried to tap messages.

Abandoned as a prison in 1971, Eastern has fallen into disrepair, and no central heating warms it. I know men who were incarcerated there and are now incarcerated at Graterford. I tried to imagine them walking along these old corridors and sitting in these cells, wondering what life was like in this strange fortress. I walked along the corridors and peeked inside a near empty cell where once stood an iron bed, a cast-iron hopper, a stool, and a rack for clothing along the whitewashed walls. Few items remain in cells that have decayed from disuse. Paint peels from the crumbling walls, and the wooden floors are long gone. Some doors and corridors remain closed altogether. Even on that dry December day, the dampness of nearly two centuries permeated the passageways. Many believe the place is haunted. Spectre or not, something haunts the prison. Inside the walls, in the hub and in the spokes of the wheel, something other than the path to reform creeps along the cold floors and into the quiet cells. I thought I saw forlorn hope disappear around a corner.

Locked iron and thick wooden doors line the long hallways. Whatever might be inside cells can retreat to dark corners—all is shut tight. At the peepholes to closed cell doors I, the visitor, transformed to jailer by my presence in the corridor, peered through and into the cells. If the "eye of God," the skylight that once gave the cells a church-like appearance, provided enough light into the cell, I could make out the shape of things. The forms morphed and transformed before my eyes. My imagination and experience created the details. My brain wrote the rest.

61

Indeed, this is the writer's work—to take a feeling, an image, a mere shadow, and bestow it with life—to put flesh on black text and a sense of place in readers' outstretched hands—to approach shared truths about being human. It is the writer's job to enter the dark passageway and open the iron doors—to risk the "sound that shall deeply pierce the soul."

Down the corridor, I moved from cell to cell, trying to follow the headphone's directions, look right, look left at the open cell. A voice, an actor's portrayal of James Morton, an early Eastern inmate, filled my ears, "In the gloomy solitude of a sullen cell, there is not one redeeming principle—the mind labors under despondency, and the imagination being left entirely to its own working increases the horror. There is but one stop between the prisoner and insanity." I wrapped my fingers around the cold iron grating of the cell door wondering if the mind longs to communicate cell to cell, as did human beings at Eastern who must have suffered greatly from their need to communicate, for they found creative ways of connecting with each other. Early inmates rapped the alphabet on walls, bed frames, and sewer pipes. Prisoners weighed notes with pebbles and tossed them into neighboring exercise yards. Ventilation flues also provided means of communication, as did the eye of God, but the skylights were nailed shut in 1852. Even though the walls are quite thick, in 1831 a prisoner could see his neighbor, another human form, through a hole he made in his wall.

At times, the brain refuses to tap out a message, with some cells remaining so quiet, dark, and hidden that not even the eye of God can shed light on them. Sometimes individuals prefer repression to memory. The brain, in many ways, is a savior in its ability to handle bad thoughts, but not for long. Ultimately, the system will fail and, as in the case of Eastern and our brains, the experiment will prove cruel and unsustainable. In *American Notes* (1842), Charles Dickens criticized the Quaker system after his visit to the penitentiary: "The system here, is rigid, strict, and hopeless solitary confinement. I believe it, in its effects, to be cruel and wrong. In its intention, I am well convinced that it is kind, humane, and meant for reformation; but I am persuaded that those who devised this system of Prison Discipline, and those benevolent gentlemen who carry it into execution, do not know what it is that they are doing."

The "eye of God" at Eastern was also called the "dead eye," which maybe is a more apt description of my and my Graterford students' internal watcher. I watch as the Graterford men struggle to bring these "dead eye" memories to light. I'm left with a question: how do we turn trauma into words on the page when the brain wants to protect itself, wants to isolate incidents and bury them deep within the walls of the prison? Once we learn how to wall off memories, we may never stop. Not only do we place bad memories in dark cells; the good memories go along with them all too often. I watch as the men struggle to remember the details of their lives, lives that they may have "floated" through sometimes because of extraordinary pain. My student Kempis says this of the trial that left him and another boy incarcerated for life at age 16:

> What I noticed when we came out of the courtroom, with the police all around us, holding onto our arms handcuffed behind our backs, I looked across and there was my family, all our family, lined up along a wall, I saw my mother, my aunt, my friends, just lined up. I don't think it really hit us what just happened. You know what I'm saying? For a long time. Matter of fact, it didn't hit me for years—what happened that day. . . . It's weird, but it didn't really dawn on me until years later, man, until years later in the cell, you know, sitting out in the yard, just pensive and daydreaming, "Yo, you got life without parole, man. You know what that means? You ain't never going home."

For my own brain, meeting it in its metaphor proved useful if not a bit alarming. That cold day in December, my brain took up the work of fiction as I peered into the cells of the women's block and listened to the echoes of my boot heels on the floor, a jailer who forgot her socks. I looked into a cell and there I was thirty or so years ago: a girl with dark hair and brown eyes and white, white skin. She could use some time in the sun. She sat on the bed with her hands in her lap and her eyes stared into the corridor. "You know more than you think you do; you'd better get out of here," she said.

As I turned to walk away, I realized that the audio was silent. I had long since abandoned the pushing of numbers to prompt it—I was far behind. I removed the earphones and wandered the corridors, wondering what was hidden in my own mind, wondering if I could lift the prisoner's black hood in this "melancholy house," a hood that Charles Dickens described as "this dark shroud, an emblem of the curtain dropped between him [the prisoner] and the living world." In the hub, I listened hard to hear a prisoner tapping a message, an S.O.S, but heard only a voice, hollow from the end of a corridor: "The prison closes to visitors at five o'clock." A figure, for a moment in sunlight, returned to shadow.

The ghost of the cherry orchard returned when I closed my eyes and stood outside against the stone wall surrounding the prison, inhaling the cold air—the springtime vision of the trees' rosy pink blossoms—the summer harvest of deepest cherry red. With eyes open, I wondered what became of all those nameless and faceless prisoners. In the years after their release, did the men and women dream at night of their cots under the dead eye, the guards outside their doors—gray, quiet souls. Did they listen to the tapping of expanding metal as water filled the radiators in their homes outside the prison walls, waiting for the message to become clear? When feeling a sudden chill, did their bodies grow stiff with fright at the memory of another cold—a lonely chill—the silent ghost of themselves?

In *Lady Chatterley's Lover*, D. H. Lawrence warns, "Slowly, slowly the wound to the soul begins to make itself felt, like a bruise, which only slowly deepens its terrible ache, till it fills all the psyche. And when we think we have recovered and forgotten, it is then that the terrible after-effects have to be encountered at their worst." Perhaps the pen is the key.

What I told the men at Graterford— and now I tell you— is this: writing allows the fractured mind to visit cells—whether we know of the visit or not. As writer Jeannette Winterson states, "We bury things so deep we no longer remember there was anything to bury. Our bodies remember. Our neurotic states remember. But we don't." We can peek in the cells and see the outlines, sometimes only an impression. Perhaps if one inmate is released into writing, more will follow. I shiver to think of those inmates whose presences are so shadowy that the writer does not know they exist. Writing *Letters* has made me and the Graterford guys

64

look in those cells for which no keys hang on a hook in the hub of our minds. We have no master key, and the process of finding the correct key for each cell is frustrating. When the iron key fails to turn the tumbler, perhaps we can pick the locks on the cells, hear the grating of the door's unoiled metal hinges, and hope that the dead eye throws light on the form inside. Those inmates who need to will run to shut the doors to protect themselves. Others may take the opportunity to come out.

"Remember," I told my Graterford students, "what one of my favorite writers, Graham Greene, says of writing: 'Writing is a form of therapy; sometimes I wonder how all those who do not write, compose, or paint can manage to escape the madness, melancholia, the panic and fear which is inherent in a human situation.'"

I looked around the room at these brave, empathetic, and altruistic men who had embarked on a journey deep into the mind's prison, and said, "When the memories come, you will be there to write them down, to do something with them, make something with them, transform them. You have been forged in fire; you have lived through some of life's most difficult circumstances, but even when so much has been taken, you have become stronger, better, kinder, braver—you've got this."

EXPERIENCE

Renée Ashley

I stuff envelopes I sit kids I hate
kids My tongue's stuck to my lip I taste glue
all the time and kid snot's on my fingers
I'd rather read a book rather be lost
in some world that isn't this one Rather
be grown-up and make money enough to

run away or at least go skating or
to the movies with a friend I have no
friends I don't talk on the telephone I
drew one on the wall in my room I call

No one answers me

*

Burger burger burger rootbeer floats and fries Inside on the grill outside hopping cars *What
can I get you m'am?* but damn it's a man
and nobody's happy now Then I get
paid in pennies to boot At nine I'm done
I have a date but I'm stood up again

It is love but not for him I'm fifty-
eight now and still think of that boy's blue-green
car and his soft hands At least he pretends
to cry when he dumps me I'm still grateful

for his gentleness

*

I'm in retail I sell Christmas balls to
old ladies who drive me nuts I hate their
assumption that balls and tinsel are my
only life Who knows what country tinsel
comes from? Not me Read the damn box you old
bat I've got a line a mile long here

at the register and the credit cards
are holding up the works Sign on the line
Mrs. Furbelow not across the slip
where the prices are Put your glasses on!

I don't last here long

*

I work the eight-to-five in the courthouse
print shop the presses running hard the thump-
thump-thump of the clamped drum clogging up my
dreams at night At six a.m. I'm toast I'm
exhausted I'm drunk on sleeplessness I'm
fucked Probably printed the ticket my-

self that I got at lunch for crossing those
double yellow lines in my car The whole
world is wrong: I should be in school reading
Proust or Joyce I should be on my fat ass

not these aching feet

*

I pump gas I'm good but I'm not sexy

and the stations with sexy girls get all
the boys But I can smile and talk how-de-
doo with the old men in Plymouths who are
too frightened of their gray wives to buy gas
at the titty stations My boyfriend owns

this Shell He's younger than I am and he
didn't go to college but he's smart I'm
working on my thesis at night: "Courtly
Love as Archetype" and by the time I'm

done he throws me out

*

Every every everyone's assistant
Typing Copying Finding primary
sources The phone is ringing It's her aunt
It's his wife or daughter It's the office:
Where's the goddamn teacher? I can't say She's
stuck in traffic He's boffing the blonde in

his nine a.m. class somewhere on the coast
in a cheesy hotel Sandy sheets Lamp
shade broken I know I've been there He'll be
back by quarter past four if he doesn't

have to stop for gas

*

On the other side of town I ghost write
for a woman who goes to the park with
her big black dog while I put in my eight
or ten hours then take the goddamned work home

because she gives it to me just two weeks
before it's due One grand a book is what

I get She gets fifteen times that at least
I'm getting screwed but it's experience
I'm owed three thousand The check's no good She's
out of town I tell the husband *I'll burn*

your fucking house down

*

The scientists are smarter than I am
but I can spell I type their papers their
letters their requisitions I teach them
where the commas go They can spell *gasi-*
fication but not *their* They're amazing
I love them all but one the slimey one

the sleazy one who offers me money
to go home with him I am appalled I
shouldn't have joked when he pulled out that wad
of bills at the luncheon Shouldn't have said

I'll go home with him

*

I've dusted battleship filters I've cut
cheese I've translated French badly transcribed
inaudible audio tapes mowed lawns
sold books And I worked a switchboard—the old
kind: woven cords and metal plugs I've walked
dogs—and OK I've kissed some crazy ass

I've been a poetry whore (that's a metaphor) I've taught fiction but this isn't
it You pull it all in It makes you You
say: There's some sort of lesson in this a

story of some kind

MOONLIGHTING

Walter Cummins

For decade or so, although I had a full-time, tenured faculty position, I wasn't scraping by; in fact, found myself digging deeper into a financial pit with each paycheck. To get by, I took on a range of moonlighting gigs I dignified by calling myself a consultant. The tasks involved writing training and procedures manuals and running writing seminars for a variety of industries. I lugged my Lands End canvas case from telecommunications to banking to electronics to supermarkets and even to a conference center. The corporate world operated on a very different pay scale from the academic. Compared with, say, grading a stack of freshman essays, it felt like free money. I wanted to give these short-term employers value for their dollars but had no investment in what they did with my labors. Nothing was at stake.

The Supermarket Industry

Now and again, I exited the NJ Parkway onto a potholed road that led into a wasteland of warehouses to meet with my contact at the headquarters of a now-defunct supermarket chain. Karen and I got on well, perhaps because she did her job with a sense of irony, bemused by the irrational decisions of the vice president she reported to and the gamesmanship of her coworkers.

One afternoon, she pointed to the row of cars parked outside her office window. "It's like playing chicken," she told me, "to see who will break down and go home first. Who stays the latest wins." I asked her if there was really that much work. "Of course not. People just read the newspaper."

She let me in on the industry's dirty little secrets, like store brands being the same products as the advertised nationals with a different label. She revealed that store managers shrugged when customers complained about finding a caterpillar in a can of corn: if you're going to put billions of niblets in millions of cans, a creature is going to slip in now and then.

I wrote procedures manuals for Karen: how to pack a paper bag most efficiently, heavy objects on the bottom, boxes against the sides; how to create those freestanding product displays that glut the aisles and block carts; how to unload delivery trucks and stack boxes in the stock room. The latter I considered my finest effort, my masterpiece, as it were. The next time I visited Karen for a new assignment, I had to ask how those manuals were doing. There were, she told me, hundreds of copies stacked in a closet. Her vice president hadn't decided when or if to distribute them or perhaps had forgotten they existed. I just cashed the check, long used to writing unread words.

Telecommunications

Like the supermarket company, the one I consulted for in the tele-communications industry no longer exists, both swallowed up by other organizations after making a mess of things. I don't take it personally, blaming the work I did as a cause of the failures. But who knows? It might have been the butterfly effect.

For this company, I both wrote manuals and taught writing seminars. The manuals involved self-instructional training in the workings of a specific industry to prepare members of the sales force to impress the client with how well they understood the way the business functioned and how they just happened to have a multi-million dollar piece of equipment that would increase efficiency, solve problems, and bring about organizational bliss.

For example, on a day I wasn't teaching, I flew out to Cleveland to spend hours with an expert who explained the ins and outs of the tire industry, he talking off the top of his head, me frantically scribbling notes with minimal comprehension. Then I went home and had a few weeks to try to make sense of it all.

I should note that this happened in a time before computers when I was reduced to writing by hand in a scrawl that took special powers to decipher. It was also a time when large organizations owned clunky Wang word processing machines lined in a room with women clicking at keys for endless hours. My handwriting was a cause of despair. The women were pleasant to my face when they asked for a translation of my marks on the page, but they must have cursed me behind my back, haunted by my script on the walls of their nightmares.

Still, they managed to process my words and turn out a manual. The next step was to test it out with representatives of the sales force that would be compelled to use it for their training and, ultimately, their corporate futures. For the tire industry manual, I flew out to Akron, a hub of radial manufacturing. We gathered in a motel meeting room, where things moved along smoothly (I won't say without a bump in the road) until the group got to my stab at demonstrating a formula dictated by the expert in Cleveland. My explanation led to meaningless calculations. Consternation. I would have to fix it.

My preference would have been to skip dinner and get right to it, but the code of sociability required that the people from the company's Akron office show off their city's nightlife. We were driven to a restaurant and then to a hot spot of that era, a disco. Within, some strange ritual was taking place. Given the overpowering beat vibrating from the loudspeakers, we couldn't hold conversations and just sat at the edge of a large dim room with a large floor space surrounded by little round tables so high that people had to stand with their drinks. When a new record began to throb, men and women paired off in the middle of the floor and gyrated under colored lights flashing across the ceiling. I tried to concentrate on what I had done to screw up that formula; but it wasn't till we got back to the motel and middle of night quiet that I finally figured it out and made the repair.

Most of my manual assignments for that telecommunications company gave me sufficient lead time, though I once got an urgent phone call pleading that I write a case study overnight because someone from a rival department would if the department that called me didn't get to it first. They'd lose power. Why not, I said, and turned the situation into an organizational dilemma that called for telecommunications to the rescue. To dramatize the case, I had to create, such as they were, characters, identifiable people with roles to play in setting up the problem and solution. On a whim, I decided to give them names from George Eliot's *Middlemarch*: Dorothea Brooke, Bulstrode, Lydgate, Fred Vincy, Mary Garth, Will Ladislaw. But my contact at the company had been an English major and changed them all to equivalents of Dick and Jane.

Writing Seminars

Helping—or trying to—employees improve their writing skills felt much like teaching undergraduates but with very different topics, even duller. My preference was to get advance samples from the people in the group so that I could see what types of writing they were actually doing and diagnose their specific needs—usually "it's" for "its," the point of a memo buried in the fourth or fifth paragraph, and sentences too glutted to parse.

The latter was most true of the examples from a company that manufactured electronics for defense systems, the prose so baroque it seemed to be encrypted. This was the group that asked me to tell them definitively whether there should be a comma before the last "and" in a series. When I told them it depends, I sensed that wasn't the answer they wanted and that they considered my inability to provide an absolute yes or no proof that I had nothing useful to say about the writing process. If one of their weapons had been handy, they probably would have vaporized me on the spot.

The greatest frustration came when I didn't have a client's samples and was reduced to generalizing do's and don't's. One such case which still bothers me involved a bank that still exists, though transformed by a series of mergers. I was to conduct the writing sessions of a week-long international seminar taking place at a country hotel outside Stratford, England, where employees from U.S. and European branches would gather. Even though I visited a lower Manhattan tower to meet with

74

several of the vice presidents—everybody was a vice president—who would be my students and even though they promised, not a sheet of paper ever reached my hands. I had, and still have, no idea for what they did.

Every instinct told me the sessions would be a disaster. They were— my hours of bogus instruction in a hotel meeting room excruciating, everyone aware I was faking it. Probably even the desk clerks out in the lobby. The air suffocated with boredom. Some of the European managers already were bent out of shape because, to fill up the complement of students, secretaries had been invited to come. You could see it in their sneers.

(Pastures surrounded our hotel, once the manor house of an estate, and the rail-thin woman from New York there to teach speech was terrified of the cows. But that's another story.)

More regularly, I conducted week-long writing sessions for a telecommunications company branch responsible for manufacturing equipment back in the days when telephones were ungainly black objects, wired to the wall and built to last 75 years. Over several years and in several locations around the country, my students were at first just middle-aged male engineers and later women managers and accountants—people who spent eight-hour days in cavernous rooms among rows of brown wooden desks, staring at blueprints or sheets of numbers, obsessed with their place in the corporate hierarchy.

The purpose of the week was more effective writing, almost all of which was internal memos and project reports, with an occasional letter to the outside world. Following their examples, I did have them sit for exercises to make them see the importance of a clear and specific subject line and an opening paragraph that compressed the gist of the message for busy recipients who wouldn't read further. Although I wouldn't think of using the analogy out loud, these openings were much like the beginning of a short story, the one chance to grab the reader.

But enforcing writing exercises on people for four and a half full days would have been a cruel and unusual punishment. So, to break things up, I revised the seminar topic to writing and communication, concocting a list of job-related issues for discussions that would fill the time between writing.

My first-day icebreaker had each person in the group stand in front of the room and explain their job function, a form of introduction. That always ended up as a litany of acronyms: "Our department processes RQTs though the BGOVs to make sure they adhere to GTW standards." Initially, I assumed I, an outsider, was the only one bewildered. But when I asked the rest of the group if they understood, I saw shaking heads. You had to be working at the next desk to get any notion of what the person was talking about. My first lesson in corporate communication.

Another involved cutting a color ad from a magazine and asking people to describe what they saw. Let's say it pictured a bucolic floral field along a sparking river as a backdrop for the product. The engineers would write something like, "In the upper left-hand quadrant there is a thick line of silvery color. The lower right is dominated by various shades of green." Someone else, most likely a person who had majored in the humanities, might say, "Spring! I feel spring! Birds in the air, butterflies, the pristine beauty of a rushing stream." Communication lesson two.

But even writing and communication lessons weren't what my groups really wanted and, I came to realize, what they really needed. They were burning to vent, and most of what they vented about related to the company's hierarchy and their place in it. The layers of management were so rigid and hermetic that employees were forbidden to communicate with someone at a higher level without the intervention of their direct supervisor. The trick they devised was the cc: list for memos. Somehow superiors could be copied but not addressed as the primary recipients. Years later, when the company eventually went down the tubes, its business shrunken, its stock in decline, its name and assets bought out by an upstart, I understood the inevitability, the other shoe dropping.

Beyond hierarchy, there was aimlessness. At one of the venting sessions a young woman in her twenties complained a project she had worked on for a year, her entire time with the company, had suddenly, without warning, been cancelled, the plug pulled. The engineers, men in their late forties and fifties, just laughed. One said, "I've been with the company twenty-five years, and not one project I've been assigned to has ever been finished."

There was a time, right after college, with no better idea of what to make of my life, I accepted a job as a management trainee and, like the majority of my classmates, might have ended up functioning as an executive in some company. Years later, well into my professing career, I made that speculation to a friend who was a corporate vice president. He shook his head. "You're too cynical." Of course. How could I not be? I'm much better suited to that world in moonlight than in daylight.

A MIDWESTERN PURGATORY

Heather Lang

The night that I saw Charlie the dog in the corner of my living room had been, up until that point, no different than most other nights. It was 2 a.m., and insomnia had struck. I thought, *Maybe if I go pee, I'll be able to fall asleep.* Mind you, I had already tried the ol' empty-the-bladder trick two, three, and then four times that night. But, anything felt better than staring at the dark ceiling of my rural farmhouse counting down the hours until I had to unwrap myself from the comforts of my quilt for the day. Once awake, I knew I would have to shiver until the warm water could reach the showerhead. Typically, this only took a minute or two, but when the temperatures were subzero and the sun was still tucked in somewhere beyond the Midwest horizon, it often felt like an entire lifetime.

During the era of the Charlie-the-dog sighting, I lived in a Wisconsin village. You know the type: the ones where you can hear the church bells regardless of where you live in town—and even if you aren't much of one for religion. Relief from those hourly clatters-and-chimes came only in the night. They were, for me, however, replaced by a ticking clock, one of chronic insomnia.

During the winter, I had two wake-up times. First, I had to rise to see if it had snowed. Waking at 4 a.m., I allotted two hours for snow-shoveling activity. If I needed more time, which happened more than once, I was out of luck (which is bad when you're the opening technician in the village's only veterinary clinic). The second wake-up time was 6 a.m., a gift from the Wisconsin snow deities—if they had decided to spare me that day.

If it had snowed, I needed to shovel the driveway so that I could get to work. And, I needed to shovel the sidewalk in order to avoid another hefty fine from the village.

These activities occurred after the shower and between at least two rounds of much-needed light roast coffee—you know, the kind with the most caffeine.

I'd broken four shovels that season, and each time I'd stake the wrecked tool into the snow bank in front of my house, in line with the other gone-but-not-forgotten shovels. To me, they had begun to look like the fence posts hosting the severed heads in Joseph Conrad's *Heart of Darkness. I had better choose my reading materials more wisely*, I thought. Although the parallel probably—hopefully!—ends here, the snow did make me feel as if I might lose my mind.

For each broken shovel, I'd offer up a moment of silence. These weren't so much ceremonies of remembrance. Rather, they were born of utter frustration. Despite not having much of a temper, after having shoveled for an hour in the dark and frigid air, and having to soon head off to work for a ten-hour shift with still-frozen feet, the broken shovels made me want to—well, they made me want to break something. Nevertheless, during these moments, I'd recoup and remind myself that shoveling was good exercise—or something.

My ex was the one who had owned the truck. The type of hearty vehicle that can, you know, handle a front plow.

I'd watch my neighbors layer their snow in a tidy corner of each driveway. Of course, they had big-tired, all-wheel pickup trucks—or whatever it is that makes a truck impressive—and on the front they'd mounted plows. Quickly, they'd removed the majority of their snow and then clean up the perimeter using hand-held shovels with the seeming ease of tying a bow on a holiday gift. I always hoped they'd offer to do a quick pass along my stretch, but never once did it happen. *So much for small-town friendlinesss*, I thought.

But, this wasn't entirely their fault. Before he moved out, my husband hadn't exactly been a beacon of warmth to the neighbors. You know that guy who'd yell, "Get out of my yard!" Yup, that guy, but the early thirties version. Of course, it wasn't entirely his fault that we hadn't bonded with the neighbors. While I pleaded with him not to cause a scene, I didn't exactly counter his actions by knocking on the neighbors' doors with friendly gestures; I never came up with excuses to say "Hello!" like borrowing sugar or bringing back homemade chocolate chip cookies or whatever it was that I should have done right.

Since my husband had moved out, I had to prioritize the numerous chores around the house. The home needed a lot of care—largely because it was old, so old that no one knew exactly when it had been built. The upstairs, which housed all of the bedrooms, had no heating system, only square holes covered by antique vents—gravity registers, I believe they were called—that allowed the warmer downstairs air to rise more naturally through them. Some days, it was as if the Wisconsin winter cackled at the gentleness of this system. The wind would whisper through the leaky, wooden walls. From its piecemeal structure, it was clear that the home had been built in stages. Perhaps one portion was the original farmhouse and another a tacked-on living room. Increasingly, after moving in, the sliding wooden doors made me think of an old-fashioned in-home funeral parlor.

Because it was even colder upstairs, and because I was the only one living in the two-story home, I slept in a room on the main floor, the one with the sliding wooden doors—largely, because I could. The marriage had been short, only one year together and another legally while trying to get divorced. "What a wild mistake!" an acquaintance would later tell me. Regardless of its length, the marriage had been difficult for both of us, and it felt good to choose my own bedtimes—and bedroom—and to leave my books in piles as I pleased, and to do the dishes as loudly as I wanted! And, not have to tiptoe around another's schedule... or heart.

Anyhow, the night that I saw Charlie the dog, I had been lying awake at two-something a.m. wondering if it would snow sometime over the next couple of hours. My mind had shifted to anesthesia calculations— not exactly counting sheep. Despite my degree in the Liberal Arts, I had since worked to earn my license as a Certified Veterinary Technician. Having never been of the math and science side of the brain, this was a rewarding accomplishment, but sometimes I worried that others would find me out, tell me that I should be writing copy or slinging coffee instead of administering and monitoring anesthesia and the like. My insecurities, however, made me particularly cautious. I told myself this was an asset. That, in the end, whatever led me to be so meticulous must have, ultimately, been positive.

Not wanting to go down that obnoxious path in my brain in the middle of the night, the one that thought about work while I should be sleeping, I dragged myself out of my old oak bed, and to the bathroom, which was just around the corner. It was my fifth if-I-empty-my-bladder-then-maybe-I'll-be-able-to-fall-asleep attempt that night. But, as soon as my foot crossed the interior threshold of the heavy wooden sliding doors, I saw him.

There, in the corner of my living room, appeared to be a scraggly, overweight dachshund mix—one that had arrived to the veterinary clinic just minutes after I had gotten to work the day before. It was Charlie. The dog. From work. In my living room. In the middle of the night. And that was impossible. Not improbable. It was literally impossible that Charlie could be sitting in my living room, or anywhere for that matter.

Charlie had been an established patient at the veterinary office. He was loyal to his mom (his owner), yet loving, almost jovial, with each member of the clinic staff. His curiosity was admirable, and, no matter how his hair was groomed, it seemed as if—within a week—his shaggy bangs would once again block his view of the world. Easily distracted by both milk bones and soft treats, Charlie might have been even more food motivated than I am. (And, this is quite the feat.) In fact, the only thing greater than 1.) his love for his owner and 2.) his adoration of food was this: his waistline.

That morning—the morning before I saw Charlie in my living room—the dog had arrived at the clinic in severe pain. He'd had a bad back for some time by then, and his owner was working toward his shedding a few pounds. Charlie was also on activity restrictions—nothing too serious, but he wasn't supposed to jump on and off furniture, nor was he to be around the other, much larger, dogs. That morning, however, the worst-case scenario had happened. Charlie had escaped his baby-gated section of the house and, in a moment of barks and excitement, he'd been trampled by one of the happy-go-lucky Labrador retrievers who lived beneath the same roof. Charlie's already injured spine was in shambles.

Once they arrived at the clinic, we injected high-end doses of synthetic opioids. But, nothing touched the piercing pain. The only ones who might have been able to help him were at the veterinary teaching hospital, which was one hour away. It was possible that, for thousands of dollars for a nerve-related surgery, a procedure with a discouragingly low success rate, Charlie's spine might have—just maybe—healed. Like many who lived in that small town within which I worked, the pet owner had very little money. Out of compassion, the woman elected to put Charlie to rest.

I was that technician, the one who cried at every euthanasia. A few owners were annoyed at my unprofessionalism, more took comfort in the company of another's tears, and many couldn't care less either way. Regardless, I couldn't help it. The tears were visceral, involuntary. Sometimes I could wait until after I'd left the room, but no matter what, they'd always come.

Charlie's passing, however, landed in my heart in an even more trying way. This is because, I thought that maybe, just maybe, I could be the one to save him. *I could drive the dog into the city*, I thought, *and put the surgery fees on my own credit card. I just might have enough room.* Really, though, the decision wasn't mine to make. Or, was it? I still don't know.

There's something that's been on my mind over the past few years. I've talked to family members at holidays, friends on nights out, and colleagues at writing events about something I can only call *the moment, or, perhaps, the moment of no return*. It seems that, when it comes right down to it, everything in life is about a single thing—an action, phrase, a decision or lack thereof, or maybe we don't even know what it is but it punches us in the gut. It's not always something like love at first sight. No, oftentimes moments mark an end. Sometimes the moment is subtle.

When it comes to relationships, it sometimes occurs long before the breakup. One friend told me that, for her, she knew it was over when she was quietly—cheerfully—singing to herself on a long flight home from a friend's wedding, and her boyfriend asked her, albeit nicely, to stop. She broke into tears. Another friend admitted that he knew it was over when his boyfriend wore a pair of shoes that he just couldn't stand. Surely, this moment was symptomatic of something greater, my friend admits. And, the significant other never knew; in fact, they stayed together for another two years. *Because who breaks up over shoes?* Those are my friend's words, not mine.

What was the moment-of-no-return for my marriage? Well, I'm not so sure that I know anymore. Or, maybe, even now, five years later, I just don't want to admit it, not even to myself. This is because it might have been the very moment that he popped the question. At an Italian restaurant, with a beautiful blue ring, my then-boyfriend asked me to marry him. I said, "yes," of course, but a week later I mustered the courage to ask, "Why blue?" These words climbed from my throat. *Because blue is your favorite color, silly*—this is what I had hoped to hear, what I had heard in my head as I practiced asking him that question again and again. Instead, however, without looking at me, my new fiancé haphazardly replied with something like this: "Because it's blue! It matches your eyes." Here's the thing, though. My eyes are hazel. Maybe green. My response? Well, I didn't say a word. I didn't know how.

Here's a moment, though, one about which I'm much more certain: the beginning of the end of my career as a veterinary technician. It was the moment that I saw Charlie the dog sitting in my living room, seemingly alive, on a dark winter night. I knew that the quirky and loveable pooch, the kind soul whose pain we had taken away earlier that day, whose heart had been silent when I had placed my stethoscope against his chest, could not actually be there looking at me. However, I also know that I saw him there in my house that night. He seemed okay, comfortable actually. And, I was not afraid. The entire exchange felt surprisingly matter of fact. He looked at me. I looked at him. I went to the bathroom, not even closing the door, and when I came back out, he was gone. But, I knew that my days in veterinary medicine were numbered. There's something about "seeing" a dead dog that changes a person.

Could I have saved Charlie? What about my marriage? That night, after I saw Charlie, I looked out the window at my broken shovels—whose own splintered spines reached toward the sky—and I remembered that I was the one who broke them.

Nevertheless, that night, the snow deities took pity on me, and they let me sleep that two extra hours.

A WRITING JUNKIE'S TALE

Bill Mesce, Jr.

I'm not one of those people who can say, "I always knew I wanted to be a writer." The funny thing is, in retrospect, it seems like I was being groomed for it long before I had any idea it was something I wanted to do in any serious fashion.

We were a working class Jersey family, but it was a house filled with books. My Uncle Pat worked for a bindery and was always bringing me things to read. When I was small, that's how I wound up with damn near every Dr. Seuss book ever published. I must've had two dozen C.B. Colby books (he wrote non-fiction for the young audience, informational stuff like *Arms of Our Fighting Men*). And, there were books about the movies: who was in them, who made them, how they were made.

My mom and dad were reading fiends. We had so many books in the house that when my brother and I would play in the basement, there were enough boxes of them for us to make a small fort.

When I was a kid, my mom threw my stack of comic books out saying they were giving me nightmares (the nightmares I have now are what they would've been worth if I still had them!). Out of boredom, I started reading their books, so, there I was, ten years old, reading Alistair MacLean's *Ice Station Zebra*.

I got my newspaper habit from my father, a bricklayer. One of my clearest memories of him: after dinner, the table cleared, he would spread the newspaper out on the dining table, prop himself on a chair on his knees and pore over every page like a rabbinical scholar.

Somewhere along the line, I started writing stories. Nothing serious, but it seemed to impress English teachers. Typical adolescent stuff: i.e.

sci fi, war movie knock-offs and the like.

I started playing around with movie-making about the time I hit junior high, intrigued by some of what I'd read in those movie books my uncle had brought me over the years. From then through high school, I'd get together with some friends, one of whom had a Super 8 camera, and we'd make short silent movies, little more than silly skits really. A few of those rolls of film are still around. I saw some a few years ago; a budding Spielberg I was not.

I went to college because my mom (my dad had passed by then) said I was going to college.

"I don't know what I want to study!"

"Figure that out later. For now: you're going!"

I had about the same amount of choice in picking a school. I went to the University of South Carolina because it was the only school on my short list that accepted me and we could afford. It was hot as hell, it was my first time away from home for more than a weekend, I was there on student loan money, and had not a clue as to what I was doing there.

I drifted through the first few years, stumbled across a few film and writing classes, felt like I had an affinity for screenwriting. It occurred to me this was something I could do; that I liked doing. I tended to think visually, and screenwriting—so it seemed to me—was simply about describing the movie I saw in my head. What I didn't learn at school was how you actually got a job doing that.

I graduated from U. of S. C. in 1977, came back to Jersey a couple of grand in the hole on my student loans, with absolutely no marketable job skills (except for typing which, in those pre-Personal Computer days, was not a common attribute), and my mother was finally thinking maybe shoving me off to college without a specific aim in mind hadn't been such a great idea.

I did some temp work. Some of it was forgettable: doing some reordering of files when a company moved. One fun gig was traveling around with this guy who set up light bulb displays for G.E. in hardware stores. I had no idea that kind of thing required a specialist.

Another time I was supposed to fill in for the morgue clerk at a local hospital during his vacation. He took me around to show me the ropes. What had been left out of the job description was that the morgue clerk was expected to help out in the morgue during autopsies, and also clean out the specimen bottles: urine, blood, tissue samples. And, since this was a geriatric hospital, there was guaranteed to be at least a couple of autopsies during the week.

"Excuse me," I told my guide. "I have to make a call." I got on the horn to my agency. "*They've got me in the morgue!*"

"Yeah, it says 'morgue clerk'—"

"*In the morgue! I'm supposed to help them with dead people! In the morgue! I am not working in the damn morgue!*"

I toughed it out for two days until they got a replacement, compromised by agreeing to clean out the specimen bottles (ew!) but no way was I going to be standing around when a body came in.

My typing skill—which, in those days, was considered impressive—kept me employed. I did a six-month stint at Prudential Insurance helping them cut and paste new rate book manuscripts together. The people were nice, the company popped for free lunch at the cafeteria, the movie studios hadn't responded to my resumes, I figured, what the hell, I could live with this. I put in for fulltime work in the department where I was temping.

The turndown was along the lines of: I was fine as a temp, but I was overqualified to do the job I was already doing because of my college degree even though it was, for any practical purpose, worthless.

Then I did a year working for an outfit called TV Compulog (whom I don't think is in business anymore) which updated TV listings for ratty little free TV guides they used to give away at supermarkets. I was promoted to head of the PBS group after a couple of months, was named Employee of the Month 11 months in, then went to see the Big Boss to bitch about the lousy pay (I think I was making $116 a week…gross… after three raises; even in 1980, that sucked).

"Bill, in just the last few months, you've received an almost 15% raise in pay."

"It comes to thirty-five cents an hour bump."

"No place else could you get a 15% raise in that short a time."

"It's thirty-five cents an hour."

Obviously, we were looking at the world from two different vantage points; one where it was always going to be a huge-sounding 15%

raise, and the other where no matter how you colored it, it was a shitty thirty-five cents, and those two worldviews were never going to merge. I left the next month.

I don't remember how I wound up at what was then Elsevier-Dutton (it had been E.P. Dutton, then Elsevier would drop them, and, while the imprint still exists, it keeps getting ingested by bigger and bigger fish; they're part of the Penguin Group now). But I thought being in publishing might somehow get me closer to being published which, so went the plan, would get me closer to a screenplay deal.

I soon learned that *everybody* in publishing thinks that (well, not about the screenplays). It's no joke that damn near every one you meet in publishing has a manuscript in their desk (ok, not quite everybody, but there's an awful lot of 'em). I was a secretary in the production department, the guys who oversee the physical manufacture of books, so I never got much of a peek at the intricacies of the editorial process. I did, however, learn a few important practical lessons:

> Very few writers make a living writing, even among those being published regularly;
>
> If you make a lot of money for the house, nobody will ever tell you your writing can improve, but if you make just enough money for the house to keep you on, but not Big Money, they're always giving you "input," "suggestions," and so on. And, if you want to stay in print, you take their input and suggestions.

There were also some larger Life Lessons:

> Authors of literary quality may talk about their art, but they'll jump to the first house that offers them bigger advances than the house that gave them their Big Break (years later, when I saw, through some authors I'd come to know, how even bestseller-scale success could be fleeting, I didn't blame them);
>
> Big Money can turn some writers into insufferable dicks (I think it's a certain karmic revenge; "I had to jump through

hoops to get here; now you can jump through hoops to keep me here).

The pay was lousy (at that time, in the early 1980s, publishing was notoriously considered one of the lowest paying white-collar professions). It was a hard job to get excited about, and I quickly learned what everybody else in the house with a manuscript in their desk learned: Being in the house didn't get you any closer to being published than being outside the house. In fact, it was inferred there was actually a prejudice against insiders (not sure I ever understood the why behind that).

By then, I'd gotten my first screenwriting gig…sort of. I was two years out of college when I'd won a screenwriting contest sponsored by the long-since-defunct film magazine *Take One* which landed me a contract with Brian DePalma. The contest involved contestants working from a scene-by-scene outline Mr. DePalma had drafted for a political thriller. After I won, signed my contract and got my very nice check, I started sending letters to Mr. DePalma (we only had snail mail in those days) asking about rewrites, about a possible novelization, and so on. After a few months of silence, I received a two-sentence note telling me my services were no longer required on the project (the resultant movie was *Blow Out*. I think I have part of a scene and a half-dozen other lines still in there, not enough to warrant a screen credit). Still, it was enough to get me my first agent who, sharpie that he was, told me he had it on good information the movie was dead. *Blow Out* was released a few months later in 1981.

Another lesson learned: you don't want an agent dumber than you.

Screenwriters don't get hired. Screenplays get bought, and the screenwriters go with them. Even when they don't get bought, screenplays are a screenwriter's calling card. My problem—and it's still a problem—was I didn't generate material. Give me an idea, a concept, an outline, I could work from that, but I couldn't originate stuff so I never had much to show around.

I was still playing with prose but I didn't consider myself very good at it. To me, it was an adjunct; if I could place a book (which, in those days, was moderately less impossible than an unknown screenwriter placing a script), a movie option could maybe get me to where I really wanted to be—writing screenplays. Well, that was the fantasy.

I had one finished manuscript: a WW II piece I'd been finagling with since high school. It had come out of more an adolescent fascination with destruction than any real dramatic inspiration. I thought it was more effective than good, but my first agent said he'd run with it…then he didn't. I never found out what that was about.

Toward the end of my second year at Dutton — about mid-1982 — I was offered an opening in a new Y/A division they were opening up. The guy heading it up liked me and told me this was one of those get-in-on-the-ground-floor opportunities. As it happens, about the same time, I'd been looking around for better paying work and, thanks to that great typing skill again, had been offered a secretarial job at Home Box Office.

I broke the news to him, told him it had nothing to do with him, he was a great guy, and yeah, this seemed like a great opportunity, but it was a question of money. The new slot this guy was offering me was going to pay about $212 a week. This was 1982 and that would almost have been a living wage for a commuter.

"I think we can come up a few dollars," he said. "Maybe go $215. How much is HBO offering?"

Even though, in title, it was a step down, HBO was offering me $40 a week more.

He held out his hand and said, "Good luck. You're doing the right thing."

While I had been at Dutton, I got my second agent. The company had contracted her to see if any dollars could be squeezed out of their backlist. I used to do some after-hours work for her, typing up her correspondence, and then, after a while, she started asking me to read prospective manuscripts for her. It was fun, but she never sold anything I liked which was probably why she didn't manage to sell my WW II book which she had taken on based on another reader's judgment that, as I remember her report, "I don't like this kind of thing, and that's why I didn't finish it, but if I did, I'd probably like this."

She was not, by trade, a screenwriting agent but she did get me a couple of gigs. One was with a couple of wannabe producers who'd somehow lucked into the rights on a post-apocalyptic novel by ex-Air Force missile jockey Douglas Terman called *Free Flight*, which had made some of the bestseller lists. They liked me because I had the pedigree of having written for Brian DePalma, yet was still enough of a nobody that they didn't have to pay me. Eventually, they sold the rights to RKO who hired me (and paid me!) to keep developing the script. On the verge of getting the project greenlit, there was a management change at the studio, the project was shelved and, I believe, it still sits in the RKO files to this day.

She got me one other paying job for a guy named Bill Persky. To my shame, I didn't know the name, but Billy was one of the great, grand men of TV, having won his first Emmy writing for *The Dick Van Dyke Show* then winning four more, including a couple for *Kate & Allie* where he was the executive producer and director when we met.

Billy was a great guy, unassuming, natural, and frank. We met for lunch (these things always happen around a food table).

"Can you write comedy?"

"I don't know," I said.

"Because this is a comedy and I'd hate to hire you and then find out you can't write comedy."

"Well, I'd hate for you to hire me and then I find out I can't write comedy."

The job was an adaptation of M. M. Parker's *Big Phil's Kid*, a Y/A comic novel about a New York teen who finds out his father is one of the biggest mobsters in the country. One scene was a funeral. If there's one thing I knew from my upbringing, it was Italian funerals; the screaming, the laughing, the things people said you couldn't believe they said:

"Hey, you know who else I heard is dead? Bennie Blue."

"Who?"

"Bennie Blue. You remember Bennie Blue. Had one brown eye, one blue eye, was on *To Tell the Truth*."

I wrote the scene as kind of an audition piece, and on that basis he hired me (ironically, that scene kept getting whittled down in the rewrites until there was almost nothing left). We worked together for about a year, but even though the movie never happened (naturally; it was one of the best things I ever worked on, though that was largely because of Billy's contribution), I came out of the experience with a great mentor, a great counselor, and a great friend.

I would spend 27 years at HBO. I started out in what was then called Subscription Information Services, which was a fancy name for the complaint department. All the calls and letters that came in to the company—hundreds per month, sometimes more — came to us, and we'd log them, tally them up and do monthly reports laying out trends, spikes, topics of interest. It had no effect at all on the company's programming and scheduling strategies because it wasn't considered scientifically valid information. I'm not sure why we did it, but the pay was decent, the benefits better than decent; sometimes you take the money and shut up.

The job had this in common with being a cop. Nobody calls a cop to say, "Look! Look! Here's people being nice to each other!" Similarly, very few people called or wrote us to tell us what a bang-up job we were doing. Oh, yeah, some did, and individual shows had fans, but most of the tonnage was griping, bitching, moaning, and venom-spewing. I was called a bigot, a corporate maggot, a Commie, a Fascist, un-American, a contributor to the degradation of women, a panderer, anti-Catholic, anti-Mormon, a porn merchant, an unraveler of the moral fabric of the nation, a poisoner of young minds, even an instrument of Satan.

After four years, our division got a new vice president, a maverick of a guy named Dave Pritchard. I could go on for pages telling Dave Pritchard stories, but suffice to say he was nuts in a fun/scary way. One time he was waiting for the elevator with a guy from the department, standing very quietly, then as soon as the doors opened, he whacked the guy in the shoulder and yelled, "*What the hell's with that shirt!*" just to see the look on the guy's face and the stunned gapes looking out from the elevator. When Dave took over the department, he called each member of the division into his office for one-on-one sessions. When it was my turn, he asked, "What do you want to do?"

"I don't know."

"You don't want to keep doing what you're doing, do you?"

"Nobody wants to do that."

"What would you like to do?"

"I like to write."

91

"Do you think you could write this corporate stuff? Press releases? Things like that?"

"I don't know. I've never done any of that."

"Do you think you could learn?"

"I could try."

"Well, let's try that. Worse comes to worse, you're back where you are, right?"

And so I was HBO's sole, dedicated corporate writer for six years. I did a little of everything: releases, speeches, executive correspondence, I even did some work on an award-winning series of Public Service Announcements the company did for Hispanic Heritage month.

Then Dave left, and some time after, I was asked to go back to my old department, but this time as manager, combining both the managerial responsibilities for the department with my corporate writing stuff.

I wound up doing that for 17 years which was probably 16 years too long. The corporate writing began drying up from almost the first day I made the move. The division staff was being replaced bit by bit with the kind of talented people who didn't need someone to do their writing for them anymore, and the complaint stuff (we were now called Consumer Affairs but it was the same old whining/bitching crap) had gotten so routine the department practically ran itself.

I was fine with that to a point; it was subsidizing my writing career. It's just that my writing career was getting less satisfying.

I'd gotten other screenwriting gigs, but they were mostly movies that didn't get made, which pushed me further out from the good paying jobs to working for a lot of small fly-by-night companies and wannabe producers. For the most part I was writing for paychecks, like the gig for the guy who called me up two days after Gianni Versace was shot and wanted to be the first guy to make a movie about the murder.

"Geez, Sam, they haven't even found the killer yet!"

"Don't worry about that. Can I get something from you in a week?"

I quit after the first draft. *The Versace Murder* was such a stinker it was never released in the U.S. Couldn't even get a cable deal. Not even direct-to-video. That's as bad as it gets.

And then even that kind of bottom-crawling work dried up.

That was toward the end of the 1990s, and I was trying to figure out how many more conversations I could stand that went like this:

"How come you run movies so many times?"

"I don't know. How come you can't read a fucking book instead?"

Well, that's how they went in my head.

By then, I had given up on my second agent, then I went through two screenwriting agents but each move only seemed to push me further out from where the good stuff seemed to be happening.

The only bright spot was that by then, I'd fallen in love with prose. I don't know how, I don't know why. Maybe as I'd gotten older I'd become a little less blind, a little less stupid, a little less…I don't know, a little less of whatever had been holding me back before. It was like being friends with a girl for a long time, and then after years of being friends, you realize, "Hey, ya know? She's The One!"

Or, it might've been I finally discovered—with painful, shameful belatedness—that prose could do what screenwriting was never going to do.

A screenwriter is a short-order cook. He may, like an Akiva Goldsman, be an extraordinarily well-paid short-order cook, even a creative one, but that's what he is. Once a screenwriter places a piece of work—it's optioned, bought, whatever—it's no longer his/hers, even if it's an original work. And once it gets into the development process, it's no longer about telling the story you want to tell, but seeing how much of it you can salvage after everybody tells you how to make it "better."

And if it's a work for hire? Even worse. You get hired because of what—so you're told—is distinctive about your work, and that's what they want you to bring to their piece. Then, as soon as you take their check, they immediately start telling you to change all the distinctive things you were supposed to bring to the property to make it less…distinctive.

Picture, if you will, a conference table. Gathered around one end are the producer (or producers), star (or stars), the director, some "creative executives" from whoever is actually putting up the money, somebody from marketing. At the other end of the table is our poor, besieged screenwriter. His/her job is to take all of the input from that other end of the table, even the stuff that's in conflict, and somehow incorporate it into something that is at least coherent. The only person at the table who doesn't get a vote on what goes into the script and what doesn't is the writer. And if he/she beefs about the direction the crowd at the other end of the table is taking…

"You know, we appreciate your commitment, and we think you're a hell of a writer, but we think we need a fresh set of eyes on this thing." Which is Hollywood's typically spineless way of saying, "Pick up your shit and get out."

But in prose, you're your own director, your own cast, your own production designer, special effects master. There's nobody telling you you have to change the winter scenes to summer, the night scenes to day, you have to cut down the cast or number of locations because of cost. You're God because you can control everything down to the weather. The only limitations on you are the limits of your talent and skill.

I have written almost two dozen screenplays professionally. While I did my best on all of them, most were mercenary jobs, and I don't think there were a handful I gave a heartfelt crap about…and most of those (thankfully) didn't get made.

I got serious about my prose. I was lucky that at HBO I had two colleagues who were both book fiends. One, J.J., was a bit of a literary snob. I don't think he ever read anybody who was still alive. His idea of buying a "new" book was to get the new translation of *The Brothers Karamazov*, or the latest Dickens edition. I'd take his cast-offs and that was my introduction to a lot of classic literature.

Michael was just a reading junkie and anything that piqued his interest he bought. I borrowed just about everything he brought into the office: Jon Krakauer's *Into Thin Air*, Dan Simmons' *The Terror*. I'd pinball between J.J. and Michael; a classic, something new, a classic, something new. And now, I wasn't just reading for fun.

How do they do this? I'm enjoying it; why? What's this guy doing? Will that work for what I'm trying to do?

I was still working—and re-working and re-re-working—my WW II novel, trying to find that key that each of these men and women had found to make the books I was reading work. I'd grown older, I'd watched the world grow older, and the novel had matured. It wasn't about explosions anymore, but about people (I would come to self-discover I'm not much of a plotter, but I do enjoy character). Still, I hadn't found a style key for it.

I was working on other stuff, too. There was a cop novel and I realized I wanted it to be less a cop novel then a picture of the New York I'd known when I'd first started working in the city in the 1980s. There was a Vietnam piece inspired by *The Bhagavad Gita* (long story, but, again, the benefit of reading to learn to write) I kept trying to wrestle into a conventional novel form until I realized *That's not what it wants to be. Stop trying to force it; it's telling you what it wants to be.* Inspired by a fable, it wanted to be a fable, and I was learning how to do that.

I started hitting the contest circuit with the umpteenth rewrite of that WW II novel (I'd found my style key reading John LeCarre) and won in the novel-writing category of the annual America's Best competition. One of the judges was an agent with a small two-person firm in New York and he wanted to take the book on.

After at least ten drafts, three agents, 27 years and (by conservative estimate) over 150 rejections, the book found a home with Bantam and was published in 2000 as *The Advocate* (its fourth title).

My agent called me up on a November night in 1998 to tell me Bantam wanted the book and was offering a two-book deal. I sat quiet on the sofa with the phone at my ear.

"I thought you'd be excited," he said. I could hear he was disappointed at my reaction.

"I'll probably get around to it," I said. "It's just that I've spent twenty-odd years learning to deal with failure. I don't know how to deal with success."

I never did quite break into song and dance because there were sour notes in the deal almost from the beginning. The Bantam deal was a case of be-careful-what-you-wish-for because Bantam didn't see the book as a stand-alone, but as the lead-off in a series. After 27 years, I wanted to be done with the material, but that was all Bantam wanted.

"I've got other things."

"Bill, we've got other authors who write that kind of material. We don't need another author who writes that stuff. But you're the only person who writes material like *The Advocate*." Which is a nice way of saying take it or leave it, and after 27 years I didn't feel I could leave it.

Which I should have. I burned out after three books, got pissy, asked to be released from my contract, separated from my agent and didn't write another word of fiction for two-three years.

That left me with just my numbing job. What had made the job bearable was knowing it was paying my way as a writer. The screenwriting had dried up, I'd taken myself out of the commercial publishing game and couldn't get back in, so now the job was less bearable. And, day by day, there was less of a job for me to have to bear.

By 2009, the company realized I was getting paid a good dollar to sit in my office and write my hoped-for next-big-break novel and watch a lot of YouTube videos. Unsurprisingly, they didn't consider that a wise investment of corporate resources. I was shown the door, so, where before I was a failed writer who still had a regular (and rather nice) paycheck, I was now just a failed writer and unemployed.

But it's worth noting that while I didn't always have the best job at HBO, my time with the company had been invaluable. Any large organization is an observatory of human behavior, a display on any variation of human dynamics. I became very sensitive to writing that got people wrong; writing by writers whose work was informed either by their own, narrow experiences, or by—worse—no experience at all.

For example, in TV and movies, corporate execs are often depicted as arrogant pricks, merciless sharks, people more brutal but less smart than the Good Guys working for them; a kind of legitimate corporate Mafia. And while I don't say they don't exist, what I learned at HBO is the world is a more complicated, shaded place than that. If there is one common thread in my fiction, it's that it lives in a moral gray area where the dividing line between right and wrong, good and bad is fuzzy, where sometimes there are no good options, and bad things happen not only because people are evil or lazy or uncaring, but also because people can be trapped by circumstance, fear, and being stuck with a menu in which all you can do is look for the least reprehensible thing to do. I wish I'd had a better career arc at HBO, but I'll never consider my time there wasted. Besides, they helped pay for my marriage, my house, my kids. I'm not J.D. Salinger; those things mean something to me (well, the house I could live without).

After my exit, I spent a year not getting interviews and realizing that not only was there no longer a place for me in Corporate America, I didn't really want to go back. Ever since I'd taken an adjunct teaching gig back in the 1990s on a lark and fallen in love with it, I'd talked about teaching as something I'd wanted to do as a second career.

My wife, always the more clear-eyed of us, put it bluntly: "Now's the time, sugar."

So, since 2010, I've been adjuncting at several colleges and universities. That's another whole story, and I've probably gone on long enough. Suffice to say that the pay is awful, the campus politics frightening, and I sometimes have students—and even, on occasion, entire classes—that make me want to go after them with a club, yet I've never done anything I've enjoyed so much, or felt so fulfilled by, as teaching…and yes, that includes writing with which I have something of a love/hate relationship.

During one of my shrink sessions, I compared writing to being a junkie: "You spend most of your time scratching around to get your fix— to sell something—then there's a short, great buzz, but then you crash and you're back to scratching around for your next fix. You get to a point where you say, This is killing me, so you quit. For a while. Then you get the itch, and you say, Ok, maybe just this one last time…"

EASTER EGGS

Kelly Jean Fitzsimmons

*M**ake it a girl's night out! Join us for some drinks and a casual Q&A about how to freeze your eggs AND the clock.*

This is what the Egg Freezing Party ad touted when it popped up in my Facebook feed. Egg Freezing Parties are today's Tupperware parties, except now women are vacuum-sealing away their potential progeny. The ad's brochure-worthy photo featured a group of stunning young ladies sipping margaritas on the beach. One blonde, straw hat cocked sassily on her head, laughed brightly. Not a care in the world. What does she have to worry about? It will be years before her biological clock starts to tick. And when it does, she can hit the snooze, secure in the knowledge that, while the eggs inside her body are withering away, the ones she was smart enough to put on ice will remain forever fresh.

In my day, the ads concerning a young woman's eggs weren't nearly this sophisticated or targeted. Although, whatever algorithm caused this ad to appear on my Facebook page was well over a decade off the mark. When I was the age of the sassy blonde on the beach, the egg ad that caught my attention was in print. There were no pictures or fancy graphics. Just a small square box appearing on the fat, ink-smeared pages of the *Village Voice*. Inside, the simple black and white lettering read:

EGG DONORS NEEDED

What caught the eye was the compensation price listed underneath—$5000.

When I answered my egg ad, I did have a care in the world, but it didn't have anything to do with planning for the future, let alone my future family. All I cared about was scrounging up my half of the rent each month for the one-bedroom apartment in Queens that I shared with my best friend.

I was 23 years old and still a B cup the morning I stripped off my clothes and folded them in a neat pile on a white plastic chair. Shivering in the sterile basement of the fertility clinic, I wrapped the hospital gown they'd given me around my body and rolled myself up onto the gurney. My lower stomach was so swollen that my skin stretched taut over the alien matter growing inside of me. The almost-life overloading my ovaries had already been sold, and I couldn't wait for the transaction to be complete.

The doctors came in and put me under for the procedure right there. Counting backward from ten, my lids grew heavy as my eyes scanned the bare walls for any small detail that would make this subterranean surgical room feel less like where they put Mulder on trial in the *X-Files*.

This isn't worth it. I want to go home. Not be probed!

Fear held my thoughts above water as I pictured little green men scooping out my eggs. Then anesthesia's dark waves pulled me under and time jumped back to where my wild egg ride began. It all started because I didn't have health insurance.

•

"I'm telling you, go get your lady parts checked for free," the girl at the party said, sipping red wine from a clear plastic cup. "You've got to get a clean bill of health before they even consider you, which means free physical, including gyno and STD screening for HIV and everything."

The thin railroad apartment was packed full of twenty-something actors, musicians, and playwrights, so this girl had our full attention at free gyno. Struggling artists in early 2001, we were still months away from world-altering tragedy. There was only horizon, nothing loomed. The most difficult thing most of us faced was figuring out how to string together enough survival jobs to make ends meet. Few of my friends had even reached for the brass ring that was health insurance. We'd all seen the egg donation ads, so we listened intently as this girl, this friend-of-a-friend, taught us how to game the system.

"You get put on this waiting list after, and it can take months to get contacted. Some people never get picked. And even if you do," the girl claimed, "you can always say no."

When I wandered into the fertility clinic near Columbus Circle in the middle of January, I told myself I was only going for the free exam. When they called me two weeks later to say I'd been chosen by a couple, I was shocked. But I didn't say, "No."

I returned to the clinic early one Saturday morning for a class on how to inject my body full of hormones. In a windowless conference room, I took a seat at a long rectangular table with a handful of other girls. In front of us, arranged like the world's most unappetizing table settings, were two kinds of needles: a simple pin-prick one and a scary syringe. Next to the needles sat a smooth, round bump of synthetic skin. We were to practice giving injections on the rubbery skin bump before taking our handy hormone kits home to jab our real skin daily during the donation cycle.

"Whether you put a packet of sugar in a twelve-ounce cup of coffee, or in a sixteen-ounce cup, the amount of sugar remains the same, it just becomes more diluted..."

The nurse leading the class presented this analogy to explain that donating our eggs didn't mean depleting a set stockpile that would render us infertile later. But that, instead of a normal menstrual cycle where the body focuses on having one egg mature and, at ovulation, releases a single egg, the drugs we'd be injecting ourselves with would create something called "controlled hyperstimulation." To put it plainly, we were shooting up our ovaries to make them pump out a crap ton of eggs all at once. When putting your eggs in another woman's basket, best not to do it one at a time.

What does any of this have to do with coffee? I don't know. Distracted by the other girls in the room, I was only half-listening to the nurse. We all looked shockingly similar: early twenties, pretty, average to tall, with long brown hair and big brown eyes. Except they were thinner than me. Surrounded by skinny doppelgängers, I practiced injecting saline into my fake skin bump. As we chatted, I learned that the other girls were mostly actresses, one was a poet, and another a painter. They were donating their eggs to pay off credit card debt or student loans. While Nurse *Coffee-talk* demonstrated the proper use of the scary syringe—insert the needle in your upper hip, pull up slightly on the plunger and check for blood, if you don't see any, inject yourself—she stressed what a wonderful gift we were giving to the women who'd chosen us. And she was right. But looking around at these doe-eyed arty girls injecting saline into their skin bumps, what if we were also creating an entire fleet of useless humans? An army of liberal arts majors with brown hair, brown eyes, and no practical employment skills?

It was an "anonymous donation" program, however, so not only would the identity of the women we were giving our gift to remain unknown, we'd also never know if the couples got pregnant. The idea of having this *maybe* child out there fascinated me. I couldn't see myself having children, so I joked about my "back-up" kid. One I'd never meet, or be given the opportunity to screw up. Everything about children was hypothetical to me back then, which made it easy to crack jokes. I spun stories about this theoretical child to make myself feel better for cashing in my eggs to put off having to deal with my own uncertain future.

The previous summer my best friend, Kristen, and I had moved to New York City to be actresses, but I was barely scraping by working as a hostess at a failing restaurant. I bided my time staring out of the restaurant's front windows at the people streaming down Eighth Avenue and scribbling lines of overheard conversations into a small notebook that I kept tucked inside the hostess stand. A few friends gave me the names of their temp agencies, but I hated the thought of being stuck in an office, and the last thing I wanted to do was go running to daddy for help. But even more than I needed the money, I didn't want to admit that I was just another wannabe actress going to cattle-call auditions and working in a restaurant. I donated my eggs for the five thousand dollars and to make myself feel different. Special. Nevertheless, here I was, in another room full of girls who were thinner, prettier versions of myself, all trying to do the same thing.

I parted ways with the other *me's* in front of the building. Brown hair streaming out from beneath snug winter hats, snow swirled around us as we shuffled off down Broadway. The fertility clinic released us back out into the wild with a box full of needles, vials of medicine, and a medical waste coffee can. The nurse also gave us an emergency number to call. You know, for whatever emergencies that may arise when you send a group of young artists in New York City home with a box full of hyper-stimulation drugs and needles.

At first, donating my eggs was this big secret I hid from everyone, including Kristen. Not an easy task when you're sharing a one-bedroom apartment and your "room" doesn't have a door. Eventually, though, it became part of my routine. Get up late. Eat cereal while watching *All My Children*. Pin-prick shot to the tummy. Pull the hazardous waste coffee can down from the high shelf in the hall closet where I'd hidden it from the short Kristen. Dispose of the needle. Put the can back. Slap on some pretty. Ride the subway into Times Square to stand for hours behind the hostess desk. Force myself to stay awake on the late-night subway ride home when the trains ran local. Fall asleep. And repeat. And repeat. Until one day I forgot to put back the can.

"Something you want to share?" Kristen asked, tap, tap, tapping the edge of my coffee can full of used needles with her manicured nail. Donating my eggs seemed better than heroin addict, so I confessed. Good thing I did, because as the donation cycle progressed from the tummy-prick shots that paused my ovaries from functioning normally to injecting the medication that stimulated egg production, I had difficulty twisting around myself to stick the scary syringe where my upper thigh meets my ass. One morning, I pulled up on the plunger to check for blood, as instructed, but stared in disbelief when the syringe filled with dark red liquid. My blood. Something I foolishly assumed would never happen.

"What's with you?" Kristen asked, walking into the kitchen. Hands shaking, I dropped the syringe, and it fell to the floor. Legs sapped of their strength, I followed.

"Blood. There's blood," I stammered, going from zero to panic, "I, there's not supposed to be blood. It's bad, very bad."

"Why?" Kristen asked, remaining calm.

"I don't know. I don't know why. They just told us it was bad. Blood in the needle is bad, very, very bad," I said, escalating to full *Rain Man* meltdown.

"But, why?" Kristen repeated firmly, taking charge, "What are you supposed to do?"

"I don't know."

"Didn't they tell you?"

"Yes, but... I wasn't listening!" I shrieked. Then burst into tears.

"Oh, for Pete's Sake," Kristen said, her voice plummeting from its usual perky chirp to the low register reserved for when she's annoyed with me. The octave I fondly think of as Kristen's real voice. "Can't you call someone?"

The nurse on the emergency line assured me blood in the needle did not mean I was going to die. Again, if I'd paid better attention during egg class, I would have known that you check for blood to make sure you aren't injecting yourself in a vein. All I had to do was pick a new spot. Simple. Except my hands wouldn't stop shaking.

"I can't do it," I said, leaning against the kitchen counter, lightheaded and near tears.

"Here. Give it to me." Kristen snatched the needle out of my hands and yanked down the side of my pajama bottoms, "Turn around."

Obeying her command, I presented my heinie. Without pause or pain, Kristen inserted the needle, checked for blood, and gave me the shot. A good friend has your back when you sell your eggs for five thousand dollars; a best friend gives you daily shots in the backside without ever asking for a cut.

"Easter? Are you freaking kidding me?" I yelled into the phone. I'd been calling the clinic daily begging them to "just scoop these suckers out of me already." Each time, the nurse reminded me that the recipient's cycle needed to sync up with mine before they could retrieve my eggs in order for the doctors to fertilize and implant them into her. I don't know anything about the woman I donated my eggs to except that her slow ovaries sure knew how to ruin a holiday weekend; my egg retrieval had been scheduled for 7 a.m. on Easter morning.

"Gives a whole new meaning to Easter eggs," Kristen snorted when I told her.

So, this is how my best friend and I celebrated our first Easter Sunday in New York City. Her attending early morning Mass at Saint Patrick's

Cathedral. Me having my eggs extracted in the *X-Files* basement of the fertility clinic. Followed by bottomless mimosas brunch around the corner at Café Europa.

•

When I woke up, it was as if the egg retrieval never happened. For all I knew, the doctors could have implanted my eggs into the little green men. When they gave me the green light to go home, I wandered, still groggy, out to the lobby where Kristen was waiting as my designated escort. We'd made it to the elevator when one of the doctors stopped me, holding out a cream-colored stuffed bunny with long floppy ears.

"A present," she said, thrusting the toy rabbit into my hands. "From the couple. To say thank you."

I held that bunny as if it was a bomb that needed defusing. *Should I cut the red wire or blue wire?* Meanwhile, beside me, Kristen was the one on the brink of explosion, stifling her laughter over my Easter-eggs bunny.

"I think I saw them. In the waiting room," Kristen said at our post-egg-retrieval brunch.

"Who?" I asked.

The bunny's black eyes stared at me with empty innocence as I sipped my mimosa. The rabbit's pink nose and black whiskers were hand-stitched, along with the flowers adorning its round belly. Judging by the quality, it was probably purchased at one of those upscale toy stores in the West Village that sold things like *Mozart for Babies* and hand-painted flashcards.

"You know, *the couple.*"

"Oh…"

Kristen, in keeping with the theme of the day, ordered eggs benedict. I got a bagel with lox and cream cheese.

"They were sitting there. Earlier, before you came out. I tried not to stare, but I think it was them."

"Did they look nice?"

"The woman, she was a bit jumpy, I guess. But mostly, they just looked normal."

I smeared an extra glob of cream cheese on my bagel and took a bite.

"They got you that bunny," Kristen said, using her toast to mop up the runny mixture of yolk and hollandaise on her plate, "they probably celebrate Easter then. That's nice."

Were they religious? Catholic? Would they have Easter egg hunts? Give her a good life? My theoretical child was a girl. The couple had to have money, at least, to pay for this. They needed my eggs. I'd given them a gift, a wonderful gift. *But what if they were bad parents? What if they were mean to her...?*

"Yeah, that is nice."

•

Fifteen years later, I stepped back into that same building off Columbus Circle for the first time since donating my eggs. This time, however, I was headed to a different clinic, on a different floor, to get my first mammogram. After I gave notice at my full-time office job to make a go of it as a freelance writer, I wanted to do everything I could, medically, while I was still covered. The mammogram was my last stop on the "do all the things tour" before I lost my health insurance. I'd picked the place off my doctor's referral list because it was close to work. I didn't even think about where I was going until the elevator doors opened a few floors before mine and I glimpsed the ghost of my 23-year-old self sitting in the lobby of the fertility clinic. When the elevator doors slid closed, she, and the years that separated us, were gone.

"Lean forward, relax your shoulders. No, relax them..."

This is what the compact nurse said as she positioned me over the imaging machine like a busty puppet. My shoulders weren't tense because I was anxious about the mammogram; hunched shoulders are my natural state of being, and, again, I was only half-listening to the nurse when she told me to relax. Instead, I was wondering if the basement operating room was still there, lurking beneath us as cold and sterile as the metal plate flattening my now D cup breast. The nurse instructed me to hold my breath. Closing my eyes as I did, I envisioned the Easter-eggs bunny staring up at me. The only creature I've ever held that was, albeit in a roundabout way, a product of my ovaries. Counting backward from ten,

I drifted off, a young girl with viable eggs. Time jumped, and I woke up a single woman pushing forty who needs to screen her boobs for cancer. I missed the middle bit somehow.

I don't regret donating my eggs, but I no longer foster any romantic notions about having a theoretical child out there. If there was a baby, her parents are the couple who gave me that bunny all those Easters ago. Now that I understand what it's like to yearn for something which seems to come so easily for everyone else, I hope I did indeed give them that gift.

When that Egg Freezing Party ad appeared, however, I balked at the idea of young women being enticed into outwitting their biological clocks before the tick even tocks. Being in your twenties is complicated enough without the added pressure of freezing-up your future. But as I reenter the life of a struggling artist, a life of uncertainty, financial and otherwise, the Egg Freezing ad also made me wonder why, back then, I assumed I wasn't going to end up having children. Did I self-fulfill my own prophecy? Yet even when I cracked jokes about my "back-up" kid, a part of me believed that once I met the right person, somewhere down the line, it would happen. It hurts to admit that the door is closed. Maybe, if I had been more like the sassy blonde on the beach, I would have slipped the doctors a couple of bucks to put an egg or two on ice for me.

Straight Job

Peter Selgin

They call it the "gap year," the year between high school grad- uation and college, when kids go off to experience the so-called 'real' world. We had a name for it, too; we called it *fucking off*. After graduating from Bethel High I didn't know what to do with myself. I was college material, but what to study? Concerning the future only two things were certain to me: that I would be an artist and that I'd be famous. I'd either be a famous actor, like Marlon Brando, or a famous nov- elist, like James Jones or Nelson Algren, or a famous painter, like Vincent van Gogh (minus the lopped-off ear and the life supply of obscurity).

Unable to choose among glorious destinies, I opted, meanwhile, to drive a furniture truck.

I wasn't hired to drive. To drive a truck that size you needed a Class-B commercial license, meaning you had to be eighteen years old or older. I was seventeen. I was hired as "driver's helper." That was my official des- ignation. I was the guy who sat in the passenger seat next to The Driver, who helped load the truck in the morning and who was in charge of reading off directions and locating streets in the road atlas, who helped carry chairs and couches and loveseats and ottomans and sleeper-sofas and beds of all sizes and fake antique pine roll-top desks and Georgian dining room sets and maple hutches and oak sideboards and copper-lined dry sinks and oak craftsman-style bookcases and Colonial grandfather clocks and all sorts of other overpriced and not terribly well-made furni- ture and accessories into private homes, apartments, condominiums, and office buildings within the four states that we delivered to: Connecticut,

Massachusetts, New York and New Jersey, with occasional forays into Pennsylvania, Vermont, New Hampshire, Rhode Island, and even Maine.

That was my *official* job. The "official" driver was Al Golabek. When Al and I first met he had a big droopy mustache and long, graying hair. He must have been at least forty, forty-five years old, I guessed. Al was twenty-eight. And since back then everyone had to have their TV show equivalent, I decided that Al reminded me of the character Rob Reiner played in *All in the Family*, the pinko/peacenik son-in-law, known to Archie Bunker as "Meathead." Except for the long hair, Al was nothing like that, really. He lived in a rustic, cabin-like house set back in the woods, had a wife and two sons, slaughtered and butchered his own meat, and was as rugged as the truck we both drove, but more reliable. On blizzard-strewn winter days he'd pick me up in his muffler-less Toyota Corolla hatchback, and we'd splutter off to Newtown, to where the Ethan Allen warehouse was located next to the town dump. Before heading to work, Al would always pull over by the dump to check for "treasures." One morning he found an antique egg-scale; another day he found an umbrella stand with just one broken piece of wood. He'd bring the stuff to the warehouse, where Bobby, the furniture repairman, would fix whatever was wrong with it, then he'd take it home. His house was full of items found at the dump.

Al, Bobby, and Stan—the warehouse manager ("Stan the Man"): those were the guys I worked with that year. They were married with kids and hairy arms and potbellies, and they drank beer and swore, and I thought, *This is the world of men*, and so it was. They poked fun at me for being young and unattached, and because they knew I would go to college eventually, as they never had, which mixed their feelings for me. *Peter the egg-head; pointy-headed Peter.* In turn I teased them about their potbellies. "Just wait till you're twenty five," said Stan, pointing at my flat stomach. "You'll probably be out to *here*." And they all laughed. Before bed that night I did two hundred sit-ups.

Depending on how far and wide, the office scheduled between ten and fifteen deliveries a day. If we finished early, we were supposed to head back to the warehouse, where Stan would make us pack the truck for the next day, or help with inventory, or do some other work. Understandably we preferred to burn up the saved time on the road. One glance at the "trip sheet," the list of stops and addresses, and we'd know precisely how much spare time would fall to us. We'd stop for breakfast *and* lunch, and make extra pit stops at Dunkin Donuts, Doughnut Time, or Mr. Doughnut, my favorite, where Margie, the cute waitress, charged us each for one doughnut but with a wink gave us two.

On summer days we'd pull over alongside a cornfield. I'd run out and come back with a load of golden ears. With luck the corn would be juicy and sweet; without it would be feed corn that we'd spit out along with our curses. All that summer long I had the runs from eating raw corn.

In weather of all temperatures, if we happened by an abandoned house we'd pull over. Al would get out his toolbox and in we'd go, like a swat team, having broken a ground floor window or pried away a plywood barrier. Once we broke into what had been a small private convalescent home and made off with a cast-iron, ceiling-mounted, oval professional chef's rack. Another time we scored a mahogany spinet piano. Whoever saw it first got to keep whatever we found. Usually Al beat me to the draw, but that piano had my name on it. It took an hour to walk it to the tailgate. Bobby did a beautiful job refinishing it. When it got to my parents' house it didn't even need tuning.

I'd been working for Ethan Allen for about three weeks when one day, after we'd stopped to get some gas at a highway station, while I waited in the cab for Al to use the toilet, suddenly the passenger door opened and Al said, "I'm sick of driving. Slide over, there, Pete." (He called me Pete.)

I knew how to drive a standard shift but had never driven any kind of truck before. And this was no small truck. This was a 45-foot box truck, also known as a "straight job," since it had a single chassis (unlike a tractor-trailer). Since it was powered by an International Harvester Loadstar 1600 engine, we dubbed it "the Cornpopper," a nickname it more than lived up to during our cornfield raids. I still remember that first moment behind the wheel, with Al sitting there next to me as I adjusted my mirrors and moved the seat to make up for the three inches he had over me. Though identical to the passenger seat in other respects—made of the same beat-up green leather—still, somehow the driver's seat felt different under me. It made me feel stronger, older and more mature. My shoulders spread wider, my arms bulged thicker, my chest swelled under my green uniform shirt. The knuckles, veins, and tendons of the hand that gripped the gearshift knob (likewise green and worn shiny) stood out more sharply than they had just a few moments before. It occurred to me then that for a moment I had lost my identity, that—had I not seen the contradiction in one of those mirrors—I would have sworn I was no longer Peter but Al; that we had switched not only seats but identities. So deep-rooted was this conviction while it lasted that I was tempted to grab Al's pack of cigarettes from the dashboard where he kept them stashed and slap one out of the pack as I'd seen him do a thousand times, and light up with his steel lighter and turn and blow the first fumes out the lowered window, as Al did always in deference to his young helper (though not always without resentment), since I didn't smoke and never had nor did I care to suck in other's fumes. Now, though, after having taken Al's place, a cigarette suddenly seemed like the most obvious and natural if not the most *mandatory,* the most *compulsory* thing in the world. In fact it seemed to me then that one could no more drive a truck without a cigarette than one could drive without, say, hands, feet, and eyes.

Cigarette or no cigarette, it didn't take me all that long to gain a sense of the mass and distance behind me, to feel as if those forty-five feet of chassis and box were an extension of the body that turned the wheel, that shifted gears, that supplied gas, clutch and break. As many an SUV driver would discover decades later, when you drive a truck you're literally riding high. You sit *above* most of the traffic, and in sitting above you also sit *beyond* the jostling fray, the madding, down-there-on-the-ground crowd. Lotus and Lamborghini drivers may prize their asphalt-gripping centers of gravity; but when it comes to feeling superior on the highway their insectine little cars have nothing over a 45-foot box truck. As Al put it, "People see a truck coming, they don't argue." Trucks invite submission; they are great levelers. They are also great enlargers. In sneakers I'm five-foot-nine, barely, average height at best, a hundred and sixty-five dripping wet pounds. But sit me behind the wheel of even a 45-foot truck and watch my dimensions swell like a sponge toy. Is this why men love driving trucks? Not so much to haul things as to extend themselves?

So I drove; I was a *truck driver*. Oh, that appealed to me; it appealed to me enormously, as did my truck driving image behind the wheel, wearing my green Ethan Allen shirt with name stitched in yellow over the left breast pocket, as reflected back at me in the truck's exterior mirrors, one large, rectangular and flat, the other smaller, round and convex, such that it accommodated not only my handsome truck driver's mug, but the whole truck sweeping back in bowed perspective, including tail gate—all forty-five feet of "her" swirled into that little round mirror like a Carvel sundae in a cup.

We took turns behind the wheel, to where Al felt comfortable enough so he'd fall asleep with me driving. Nothing could have pleased me more: That he could trust me that much, that he could feel so *relaxed*. It helped me relax, too. Too much, in fact. One day I started nodding off at the wheel, and would have nodded straight across the divider and into the opposite lane had Al not woken up and grabbed the wheel in a nick of time. "Pull over," he said, and I did. Al chewed me out royally, to the point of tears. "What, are you *bawling*?" he said, for sure enough the macho trucker had suddenly turned back into a seventeen year-old boy, a barely mature one at that. For nearly nodding off at the wheel Al would soon forgive me; for crying—that would take longer.

It took three weeks, in fact, and a cracked bell housing. The cracked bell housing belonged not to the Cornpopper, but to a Penske rental truck we'd rented from Eddie's Sunoco Station, while Eddie (who we called "Half-Faced Eddie," or just plain "Half Face," the other half having been scorched away years before by an engine explosion) did a ring and valve job on the International. We discovered the cracked bell housing soon after making our last delivery of the day: two end tables and a cuckoo clock to a customer in Mill Plain. We were coming down a narrow, steep, ice-slick road. Aunt Hack's Lane was the name of the road. I still remember. Who wouldn't? The truck's brakes were just about gone, too; so were the windshield wipers. The same stubborn patches of ice held on from morning till dusk. Because the brakes weren't worth shit, Al had been using the transmission for a brake. All day it had worked fine. But now, as we careened down the icy hill, for some reason the transmission wouldn't downshift. "Hold on, Pete," Al said and applied the emergency brake. Instead of slowing, the truck's wheels locked and we skidded.

It's a good thing I wasn't driving; I'd not have known what to do. But Al did. He released the emergency brake, forced the transmission into neutral and then, with a nasty sound of metal gears tearing at each other ("Hey, grind me a pound!"), rammed it into second. The truck protested, bucking and lurching, but our momentum was slowed. Using a combination of emergency brake and clutchless shifting, hearts in throats Al got us down *ugly* Aunt Hack's Lane.

Instead of returning to the warehouse we drove the truck back to Half Face and told him about the bell housing, that he had to give us another truck. Half Face shook his scarred head. The hair on the good side of his skull was shiny and blond; on the bad side it was crinkly and dull-red. "Can't do," Half Face said. "I'm booked out of trucks until the New Year. You'll have to take her to Bridgeport." Bridgeport was where the Penske truck depot was located, forty minutes away down Route 25, a sporadically lit, narrow winding road, prone to fog. And it was foggy that night. And dark.

From the Sunoco station office Al phoned the showroom and told the acting manager, I'll call him Ron Stillmann, about the rental truck. I stood outside. From where I stood I could barely make out the shapes of the pumps, the fog was so thick. Through the window I watched Al grow more and more agitated, his forehead darkening as it did when he got angry.

After a few minutes he came out.

"He wants you to go to Bridgeport," Al said. Emphasis on you.

"I can't; I don't have a license. Remember?"

Al shook his head. "He knows, Pete. And he doesn't give a shit. He's got fifty customers threatening to cancel orders if they don't get their furniture by Christmas. If one of us doesn't go he'll fire both our asses. And I'm not going."

"You said I'd go?"

"I didn't say anything, Pete. You don't have to do anything as far as I'm concerned. As far as I'm concerned he can fire me. Go talk to him."

None of the people I worked with at Ethan Allen liked Ron Stillmann.

Even as a funeral parlor director, his job before coming there, he had apparently not been well liked, which says a lot. At the showroom he'd hit on the saleswomen and receptionists, telling bawdy jokes and inviting them for rides in his Jaguar, making their lives impossible when they refused. He had his eye on the manager's job. Frank Trimborn was the manager. And though Frank drank too much and was over-generous with bonuses and free furniture ("*That* chair you want? I wouldn't let my neighbor's dog shit on that chair. Do me a favor, would you, and take it away!") Frank had a big heart. When not working at the showroom, he was President of the Bethel Theatrical Association, which every summer in a building it leased from the Veteran's of Foreign War produced revivals of Broadway shows, a couple of which I had leading roles in. Frank got me the driver's helper job. The morning after Thanksgiving day, with too much turkey and wine still in his estimable belly, he walked through a glass door. Since then he'd been recuperating. Ron Stillmann was in charge.

For myself I didn't care, but I wasn't going to let Al lose his job. He had a wife and two kids.

I talked to Ron. I waited until we were back at the warehouse and called from there with the others all gathered around and watching. I told him exactly what a huge pus-dripping dickwad he was but that I would drive his goddamn truck for him and Merry Fucking Christmas to you, I said, and slammed down the phone. The others were impressed. Their jaws hung. They patted my back. "Way to go, Pete."

But I was already on my way to the truck thinking fuck them, fuck everybody. Stillmann wants his truck exchanged, I'll exchange his truck, sure, no problem, I'll exchange it. Fucker. Cocksucker. I climbed into the cab, started the engine, grabbed Al's cigarettes from the dashboard and lit one. Fuckers.

I took off. I slammed gears and hauled butt down that foggy dark road, high beams on the whole way: the fog sucking up most of the light they threw off. I was livid, afraid, tears and cigarette smoke in my eyes. I wanted to mash that truck into Ron Stillman's face, but I also wanted love: the love and respect of other men, sure; but mainly I wanted to love myself as a man, a fully grown man, to feel at last that I had not only arrived at but gone beyond the crux of manhood. This truck with broken bell housing that I drove, it gave birth to me that night, to a Peter who was and wasn't me; to the Peter who could drive a crippled truck forty miles to Bridgeport in the fog and ice with bad brakes. To the Peter, more or less, who writes this today.

I shifted gears; I played the radio; I lit another cigarette; I came of age.

When I got to Bridgeport, a man was there waiting in the Penske lot to greet me, to give me the keys to the replacement truck. I had to pull the injured one into a narrow slot between two other rental trucks. By then I was so tired I could barely think, let alone back a forty-five foot truck up into a space as tight as a toaster. I didn't even hear the sound of iron against aluminum as the tailgate of the truck I was in did a *Titanic* against the iceberg of a truck to my right, only this time it was the iceberg that bought it: a gash nearly the whole length of the box and in places two inches thick. *Fuck 'em if they can't take a joke.* By then though I hadn't even found the replacement truck in the lot and already I was halfway home. I didn't care what I tore up along the way. Who says grown men aren't destructive?

A few weeks later Ron Stillman called me into his office and showed me the Polaroid pictures he'd been sent showing the damage. He said he'd have to take it out of my pay. I said that would be difficult considering that I quit. And then I threw the keys of the truck down on his desk to which I gave a solid kick before leaving. As gestures go it might have won an award for hollowness, since by then it was January, and I had been accepted for mid-term enrollment at the Pratt Institute, where I'd decided to study painting and drawing. School started next week. Brooklyn, here I come.

And that's my story. Except that two years into Pratt I decided I wanted to be a writer, so I treated myself to another "gap" year, during which I did many shit jobs, though none quite as manly.

INTERNSHIP AT TIFFANY'S

Julie Anderson

Even if you haven't seen *Breakfast at Tiffany's*, you probably know the opening scene: Audrey Hepburn emerging from a yellow cab, wearing a long black evening gown with a quadruple strand of pearls around her swan-like neck, making her way to one of Tiffany's windows and gazing longingly at the diamond bracelets displayed inside.

The allure of Tiffany's is indisputable. As a child, I used to love going on trips with my mother and sister from our tiny Bronx apartment all the way down to 57th and Fifth to see my mother's friend, an employee at the famed jewelry store. The emeralds, sapphires, and rubies glittering in Tiffany's display cases mesmerized me. But what really got my attention were the diamonds, especially the Tiffany Diamond, perched in its own special case inside the store, embedded into one of the walls behind a thick pane of bulletproof glass. The Tiffany Diamond was a huge, 128-karat affair that threw off every color imaginable. I'd stare at it, lost in its endless refractions of light, until my mother eventually had to drag me away.

Almost as fascinating to me as Tiffany's diamonds were the people who bought them. Who were these elegant ladies who brushed past me, perusing the display cases as casually as if they were shopping for dinner? At Christmas-time, these women wore fur coats and heels and somehow they just looked like money. My mother was beautiful, too, but even as a small child, I could tell the difference between her fake fur and their real ones, between her self-styled hairdo and their expensive coiffures. These women carried themselves differently—chins up, eyes down—and though I loved my mother absolutely, I nonetheless harbored the classic childhood fantasy of having been switched at birth. Someday, or so the fantasy went, my parents—my real and enormously wealthy parents—would come to claim me.

Thanks to my mother's becoming a secretary at one of New York City's private schools and my getting a scholarship there a few years later, I got closer than the average girl from the Bronx usually gets to that world. While this experience made me intellectually ambitious in a way I'd never known possible, it also had the unfortunate side effect of strengthening my desire to become one of the rich ladies I used to gaze up at in Tiffany's. At my new school, I quickly acquired many friends who were bona fide members of New York City's elite, and from them I learned how to "pass" for rich. I toned down the Bronx accent, favored flannels and loafers over tight sweaters and sequins, and, above all, never ever talked about money in front of those who had it. This last lesson was learned early on in 7th grade—my first year at the private school—when I visited Jackie Friedman's Park Avenue apartment and commented on everything from its size (the elevator opened into an apartment that spanned the whole floor) to the fact that she had a maid whose room was bigger than the one my sister and I shared. I was never invited back and Jackie quickly dropped the friendship. It was a lesson I never forgot.

In 1986, the summer after my first year at college, I got an internship at Tiffany's thanks to my mother's friend. Liz, a pixie-like woman with silver hair who'd come over on the boat from England with my mother in the early sixties, never simply entered a room; she swept into it, enveloping you in a cloud of expensive perfume as she embraced you and gave you a kiss on both cheeks. Liz always dressed stylishly, looking every bit like the rich women her company catered to, even if she'd started out as a poor, working-class London girl.

When I found out about the summer job Liz had procured for me, I didn't see it as an entryway to the business world—as my mother had hoped—but, rather, as a means by which to study more closely the women whose ranks I aspired to join. I pictured myself behind the diamond counter, reverently handing these women million-dollar necklaces. They'd try them on, glance at their silent, gray-suited husbands for approval, then admire their own sparkling reflections in the mirror. *One day*, I thought, *I'll be one of them.*

The reality of the job proved radically different from my fantasy; I was put nowhere near the display cases nor the customers. Instead, I was discreetly tucked away in the Pearl Department on the sixth floor, in a tiny cubicle of an office with two women, one named Jane, the other Katie. I'm guessing I was put there because Jane and Katie didn't have much say and besides, the higher-ups figured a clueless nineteen-year-old couldn't do much harm there (since I had virtually nothing to do). Fortunately, the two women welcomed me as an interesting distraction.

Jane and Katie were, in fact, just a few years older than me. Like me, they were both blonde and trim, but neither shared my ambition to write and travel nor had they grown up in the snobbish private school world of New York City. For these reasons, I looked down on them, failing to understand the one true difference between us: they were rich and I wasn't. My family constantly teetered on the brink of bankruptcy, in large part due to the expensive private school tuitions that my sister's and my scholarships didn't fully cover.

Though I didn't deserve it, the two young women treated me kindly. Jane, the quieter—and to my mind—more elegant of the two, was more of a mentor to me than Katie. She taught me straightaway to say "Tiffany," not "Tiffany's." This was strict company policy. For some reason I never could fathom, but that made complete sense to Jane, the possessive "s" was in very poor taste. In addition, Jane had an uncanny ability to tell a good pearl from a bad; whenever one of the vendors came up to the office—usually a Hasidic man with a long beard and dark suit—he'd open up his briefcase, pull out a thin black tray of pearls, then set them in front of her.

"No, no, no," she'd say, inspecting them lightning fast, with a palpable disdain in her voice, until she came upon a strand that made her pause. "Maybe," she'd remark. "Leave it here and I'll think about it."

The man would nod, sometimes fawning, never protesting. As a buyer at Tiffany's, Jane might have been young, but she still commanded respect.

Afterwards, she'd sit with me and explain what made some pearls better than others. She'd hold a strand up to the light, pointing out its virtues or defects, but I never could see them, no matter how hard I tried. Jane gave me article upon article to read, but nothing really helped. I learned in one magazine that true pearls—all of which are cultured these days, some higher quality than others—are grainy if you bite them, so when I was alone in the office, I'd sometimes scoop up a particularly expensive strand and stick it in my mouth. While I never could tell much of anything that way, I have to admit that some latent, subversive part of me enjoyed knowing that I had a half-million-dollar pearl necklace wedged between my teeth.

Sometimes, Jane, Katie, and I would try on the necklaces, modeling them for each other. We'd prance around the tiny space, wearing pearls worth hundreds of thousands of dollars, which we weren't supposed to do, of course—not only because it was unprofessional, but also because pearls decay over time, especially when they come in contact with your skin. (Oils hasten the decay of a pearl's nacre, the substance that gives a pearl its gloss. It's this coating—secreted by oysters—that's a pearl's true essence, not the little plastic bead at its center.)

These were the highlights of the job, but mostly, I just sat around and filled out vendor forms to keep track of which pearls were bought by Tiffany's and which ones were returned to the long-bearded men. It was, in truth, excruciatingly boring and my boredom was compounded by the lack of what I deemed compelling conversation in the office. Not only were Jane and Katie not interested in books or ideas or politics, but they didn't seem especially interested in travel, which I yearned for. Only one topic truly interested them: weddings. Jane had recently gotten married and planned to move to Connecticut to start a family with her new investment banker husband. Katie, by contrast, was unmarried and her anxiety was palpable. At twenty-four, she was a whole year older than Jane, but her man, also an investment banker, still hadn't popped the question. The two women speculated non-stop about when and where this might happen, and when it finally did happen, there then ensued endless talk about the wedding: Where would it be held? When? Which caterer? What style of dress? And, of course, what jewelry?

On the one hand, this discussion turned me off. During my first year at an intensely academic, left-leaning university, I'd learned about the male gaze, patriarchy, the objectification of women. I'd heard Betty Friedan speak about the media's war on women's rights, and I imagined myself a feminist. On the other hand, I was captivated by Jane's and Katie's wedding talk, envious of it, even. The part of me that aspired to be a Tiffany's customer—one of those elegant women with a gray-suited husband—readily imagined my own wedding one day to just such a man.

I had one in mind already. Jon was a kid from the Bronx who'd dropped out of college at nineteen and, at twenty-four, was still living at home. Though he might not sound like rich husband material, he was already climbing the ladder at Goldman Sachs—the "Harvard" of investment banks, as he liked to put it—and commanded a six-figure salary that was rapidly growing. When he described to me the thousand-dollar shoes and lavish lunches, not to mention the multi-million dollar salaries of some of the older men (yes, they were all men at "Goldman"), I listened with rapt attention. It was one thing he and I had in common: a fascination with the rich.

It would not be an exaggeration to say that I worshipped Jon. Not only was he five years older than me, but he was handsome, sharp-witted, and cocky as hell. (At fifteen, he'd created a knock-off version of a well-known video game and sold it for half-a-million dollars. Atari sued him and he had to pay the money back, but he just found the whole thing funny.) When Jon said he was going places, I believed him. I secretly dreamed of climbing the social ladder by his side, but, problem was, I quickly lost myself in his presence, becoming tongue-tied and awkward and shy. Plus, I was his kid sister's best friend, and it was strictly verboten to date my friend's adored big brother. Still, Jon seemed to like my company and I sometimes wondered, though I scarcely dared hope, that he might feel the same way.

That summer changed everything. I went on a disastrous blind date with a man—also about five years older and an investment banker—whom Katie had set me up with. When I told Jon afterwards how the man had made pass after pass at me during the course of a two-hour dinner ("So, young Julie," the man had leered, pointing to a hotel as we walked down Park Avenue, "is it true what they say about Catholic girls? How about we go up for a quick visit and see?"), Jon became livid, but also got the point that I was no longer a kid. Soon after, we started sleeping together. It was a secret between us and though we never actually discussed the reasons for the secret, of course I knew my friend would be pissed. What I didn't know, however, was that our relationship was also likely to piss off my friend's mother, who only wanted her children to date Jews, if they absolutely had to date anyone at all.

It was a tricky position to be in: I wanted to tell the world I had this wonderful new boyfriend, but couldn't. Still, I must have hinted at something to Jane and Katie; they exchanged knowing looks and I could sense they approved. Goldman Sachs was, after all, a fine place to go husband-shopping.

At the same time that I delighted in my first real boyfriend, feeling like I'd won the lottery or accomplished some great feat, the incipient feminist in me began to emerge and started sabotaging the relationship. I couldn't reconcile my opposing feelings; I was simultaneously proud and disapproving of Jon, impressed by how much money he made while also critical of how he made it. Even more so, I was critical of myself for admiring Jon's job, for wanting to latch onto him and his money. As these two sides of my nature—feminist and husband-seeker—battled for ascendance, yet another part of me looked on, bewildered. Who was I? The budding intellectual who aspired to travel and write and do things for herself? Or the snobbish intern at an expensive jewelry shop, biding her time and playing at a job till she got married, had kids, and settled into her safe, pampered life? I shudder now to think what a nightmare girlfriend I must have been as I lurched from one dramatically different image of myself to another.

Perhaps, though, this is what being a young woman is all about, at least in modern America. Such wildly different messages are given to women all the time about who we should become: confident, independent women or pretty, helpless princesses. Of course, it'd be nice to think that the princess dream is dying away, but I don't think that's true. Little girls still love dressing up as them and our new First Lady is nothing if not a grown-up version of a princess. It makes sense that the fantasy is thriving: it's a powerful marriage of gender and class, of consumerism and the American Dream. If you're moderately pretty, pleasing, or charming, maybe you, too—with some artful makeup and clothes—can marry a man who'll take care of you and bedeck you with jewels for the rest of your life.

But the thing about dreams is they're precisely that: dreams. I'm thinking back to the opening scene of *Breakfast at Tiffany's*: Audrey Hepburn staring in the window, looking at the jewelry while she sips her coffee and munches her pastry, the dreamy notes of "Moon River" playing overhead. For a moment, Hepburn—in the guise of her character Holly Golightly—lifts her eyes and cocks her head, seeming to meet the viewer's gaze from behind a pane of glass. In this iconic shot, with pearls draped around her neck and diamonds nestled in her swept-up hair, she represents everything that Tiffany's itself has come to stand for: beauty, elegance, mystery, wealth. (Indeed, her image and that of the store are virtually synonymous now.) But Hepburn dares us to see beyond the image, to the truth that lies behind it. And the truth of it is this: Holly Golightly is a penniless young woman on the outside looking in, longing for a world she will never have.

No doubt Truman Capote, who wrote the original novella, was commenting on the American Dream here, tipping his hand to *The Great Gatsby*, the novel that, more than any other, explores the complexities, contradictions, and false promises of that dream. And it is *The Great Gatsby* that, perhaps, has the final word on class, on those who occupy the top of the American social hierarchy and live the so-called dream. When, at the end of the novel, Nick Carraway walks along Fifth, he encounters Tom Buchanan looking in the window of a jewelry store. They shake hands, then Tom goes into the store to purchase a multi-million dollar pearl necklace or maybe a pair of cufflinks. It's this image—of Tom entering a store that is quite possibly Tiffany's—that I haunts me: Tom—the racist, sexist bully of the novel whom everyone despises for his small-minded cruelty—is the truth behind the gray-suited man I'd dreamed of marrying. And Daisy—vain, manipulative, and bored out of her mind—is precisely the woman I aspired to be. (There's perhaps another reason this image from the novel bothers me: I can't help but note how much Tom "frowning into the windows of a jewelry store on Fifth" reminds me of the current President, a man who built his flagship hotel right next to Tiffany's and even named his second daughter after the store. Trump, perhaps more than anyone, knows how to capitalize on images, especially the one that Tiffany's projects. The parallels between him and Tom Buchanan are nothing if not striking.)

That August, my internship at Tiffany's ended and a year later, Jon and I broke up. I wound up on the West Coast, where I got a PhD in literature, teach at a school not unlike the one I attended, and live with a man who's smart, wonderful, and makes about the same amount of money I do. In other words, I've found what you could call an intellectual, feminist life and I'm happy with it—more than happy, in fact. And yet, when I return to New York, I'm sometimes hit with a pang of longing. Despite everything, I can't help but feel the pull of that old, deep dream, the one Tiffany's capitalizes on so well. I might even find myself heading down Fifth and staring in the windows of my old workplace, wondering with some wistfulness if Jon has become one of those gray-suited men who accompanies his wife, a woman like Jane or Katie, into Tiffany's, waiting by her side while she pauses over the diamonds, selects one, then has it wrapped up in a pale blue box with white ribbon.

ON THE BEACH, WORKING, WAITING

Kevin Carey

> So the immortals spun our lives that we, we wretched
> men live on to bear such torments..."
>
> Homer, *The Iliad*

That year I picked forty-eight thousand pounds of lobster, picked it, cut it, squeezed it, two hundred and fifty-two days (about one hundred and twenty pounds a day), the lines in my hands outlined in red and each day my fingernails packed with enough white meat to stuff a ravioli.

I chopped the celery that got mixed with the lobster, stocked the rolls that the lobster went in, loaded the grill where the lobster rolls got toasted, filled the pickles and cut open the boxes of chips that went on the plates that the lobster rolls got served on. When you took that roll away from the counter with your pound of meat, celery, mayo, chips, pickles, on a ten-inch cardboard pie plate, covered by aluminum foil, tucked in a small white paper bag, I was all over it.

•

I had history here. First onion rings, then the counter, then frying fish and clams, then setting up plates of food, or sometimes slicing roast beef. I moved through the stand like a utility infielder, playing nights and days and weekends and mornings. You name it, I did it. Set it up, pushed it out, fried it, cooked it, bagged it, cut it, breaded it, collected for it, and cleaned it. Fifteen years, all hours, all days, I did it.

•

Any midnight and the beach could still be cooking with gas, head-lights from one end to the other, muffled hip hop from tinted windows, a Harley or two weaving in and out the traffic, the city skyline looming. The beach people, doing beach things.

There's a recipe to beach life: salt air, fried food, sun tan lotion, traffic, kids drinking beer on the seawall, sea gulls picking trash, girls from the Ave in cut off jeans, hot August nights. People living on the beach are a part of a grand design. Behind the moaning and the groaning and the bitching and the drinking and the hangovers and the fights, they know there is something driving them to do the things they do, a strange serendipity they see in the ocean, in the seasons, in the storms and the waves, in the high and low tides, when the water washes up over the sea wall in winter and the sea smoke dances off the ice packs.

In the summer, a steady stream of bikinis, elderly a.m. walkers, hard-core heads in Bob Marley T's, bikers, hot rods, arcade pigeons, cocktail captains, tan hunters, immigrants, Americans, young ones, old ones, fat ones, skinny ones, lines of motors idling, music blaring, waiting, waiting in line, waiting in cars, waiting for the tide, waiting for the sun and the seafood and the beer and the taffy and the old days, the new days, the easy lay, the cops to kick them off the sea wall at midnight, and us, a broken band of misfits waiting to wait on them.

I watched it all go by, sometimes at work, sometimes out the bar-room window lined with sea shells. No sense heading home. No one to go to, just this beach, people who worked it, who played on it, people who didn't smell you or look you up and down because you had dried white flour and sawdust on your shoes, the walking talking fish plate, the french fried human onion ring, stamping two inches of flour off his high cut sneakers. The beach brought us all together, a long line of accumulated misery.

Throw a few back, that's the ticket. If he's buying, I'm flying. Put it on ice, Marie. I'll get to it, sure as shit.

And then some, and the comfortable sway back in the legs, the one that makes me think I can dance and shit if it don't go down better after eight hours in the box. But there's more to come, always, more work in

124

the morning, more cooking to do, more bums to wait on, like the disco ball says, more more more.

•

I was a set up man too, heard things, things like: three fish, small clam, scallop plate, two medium fries, three small rings, fish dinner, four clam plates, fish sandwich, small fry, shrimp plate. Hours at a time, lunch time and after, ten or twelve window guys yelling, fried food, plates of it, denizens of the deep. Many tried this job, the ones who did it best drank the chaos like alcohol, the more they had, the more they wanted, the more they heard, the better they got, found their groove in the late innings, a fourth quarter running back, treated the voices like inspiration, customers yelling at window men, window men yelling at them, them yelling at fry guys, voices littered around their heads. Me, I got orders on the brain, had seafood nightmares.

•

If you spent the day sifting buckets of cornmeal and white flour, breading shellfish with your fingers, clams, scallops, fish they think is haddock, you'd throw a few back wouldn't you? If you walked the side-walk smelling like corn meal and Canola, the last nine hours of your life staring into several hundred fry baskets full of french fries, staring at a long line of beach bums, you'd head for your favorite arm rest and throw down a couple of what the doctor ordered. Jesus Christ, who wouldn't?

Over the years conversations from various pay phones in dark hall-ways of various barrooms. *Hey Baby, What's up? Want some pizza? No? Not hungry? What? Is it that late?*

And back at the bar ordering two more. Why two?

Because by the time I drink this one I'll want another and you might be busy.

•

Sometimes after work when I got a fog on I remembered the musty smell of an early morning gymnasium, stretching the warmth into my body, the cold wood floor, the bleachers, the dust in the corners, the leather ball, the thick air, the squeak of well-worn sneakers, the groan of wind sprints, the joy of shooting, the flick of the wrist, the touch off the glass, the suspended time of a long range jumper.

Or the games, sixteen one night, twenty another, always once or twice stepping into a passing lane, picking someone clean off the dribble and pushing it up court, slowing that last sure step, *in my house now*.

I might remember two free throws in Boston Garden, the closing seconds of a State Tournament game, my father in the stands praying, as if it were a dream, a dream worth the years of shoveling a court in winter, shooting with finger-less gloves, dribbling miles around the neighborhood before school, and shooting and shooting and shooting, and then what? Then I left it like a tool bag at a job site, left it sitting and rusting in the rain until it was just something I did, something that didn't work anymore, something, like my job, I lost ambition for.

•

It wasn't the work, I liked the work sometimes, it wasn't the guys, I liked the guys sometimes, it wasn't walking down the boulevard like a man on death row, it wasn't smelling like onions when I ordered a beer and something short and hoped some long-legged baby would tuck me in for the night. You know what it was? It was nothing, nothing but the day I said fuck it. A sunny August day, rolls loaded on the grill, condiment trays filled, early morning walkers served, and a guy smoking a cigarette against the sea wall, smoking, taking a sip of a large coffee, cream no sugar, the gray smoke blending with the haze, and it dawned on me, just like that, a frozen moment against the sea wall, and I realized I'd had enough.

•

There's a certain place for a song, not every song, but one that comes at the right time, when the mood of the strings fits your life, some candid vocal that slips into your soul, a ballad that evokes the consensual damage in all of us, talks about things we've missed or forgotten or in the most dangerous places, things we remember.

The silence of a falling star...

An outdated jukebox, probably still had quarters from the sixties floating around in its belly, a weird cross-section of American music, a little disco, some rock, some one hit wonders, and some country, cut off somewhere around 1970. The title cards were yellow and curled at the edges. But it played and the regulars that came to the basement "no tell" tavern still fed it on occasion, but usually they waited for me to do it, a perk for coming to the bar in the first place, the purple-light glass front crescent bar, where I hid when I wasn't working a "peep show house" construction job in Boston's combat zone.

lights up a purple sky...

You could call this the beach, but it was the end of the strip, the demilitarized zone. It got some beach people, but not many, mostly people who wanted to be on the fringe without waiting in the summer traffic or dealing with the bikers or the punks or the girls strutting their stuff on the nights hotter than griddle butter, nights when the old women from the Ave lifted their house dresses to their knees and waded in the ocean, watching the planes fly low to the airport, and people slept with their babies on the open station wagon backs, and always someone drank too much from a brown paper bag and started a fight. In here, it was safe and air conditioned and the drinks were cheap, and the people behaved, some sucking pineapple cocktails, other nursing twelve-ounce beers, the bottle sweat forming pools around the damp napkins and mostly there was chatter and jokes and whatever extra nonsense some half a doper wanted to tip me with.

the moon just went behind a cloud...

I always played it before I opened, while I was wiping bottles left out over night, cutting fruit, smoking a cigarette with a Kaluha and coffee. Might as well be with my people on the slow burn to midnight, beer and butts, booze and pretzels, a scotch or two, something green with Midori or one of the Russian brothers in a shaker, something to soothe the ills of life near the beach, something to remind me that Hank Williams was a real country star who died at twenty-nine years old, drunk in the back of a car on route 66.

I'm so lonesome I could cry.

*Translation by Robert Fagles

WITH ANY LUCK

Letisia Cruz

A rut is a revolving door.

A black swirl emerges on the fabric. Mike is holding the spray gun against a grey t-shirt. Paint fumes circle the walls. The girl and her friend cough, then stare at Mike's ass and giggle. Mike is a good-looking Puerto Rican with two kids and a pregnant girlfriend. He half-smiles and the girl scribbles her phone number on a brown paper bag. Within a minute, girl names in  black and blue graffiti spread across the back of two shirts. The girls each hand me $20. I bag the spray-painted tees and handwrite receipts. After the store clears, I open the register and divide the money equally. Then I wipe down the counter and reopen the front door. Never ring up cash if the boss is out—that's the rule.

A rut is a well-worn track.

They move me out of the perfume department on account of my sales record. My boss points out that everyone has different strengths—says I'm better at stocking shelves than at dousing customers in toilet water. But shelves depress me on every level. The day after photo girl quits, I make my way into film. I stand over the wheel and watch the photographs emerge. The Kodak machine sits near the storage room where gallons of color developer beg to be unleashed. On day one, three customers complain about my generous reds. *Bright sunlight can lead to harsh pigmentation*, I lie. I silence the critics with coupons and adopt a more conservative approach to magenta. Suddenly, I'm employee of the month.

A rut is a repeated pattern.

Bean burritos are my favorite thing to stuff. For starters, I don't have to touch the meat. Once the frozen bag of beans is cooked, it's only a matter of spreading. The crunchy tacos are trickier and crack every time I fill them. *How many times do I have to tell you to use less cheese?* my boss asks.

A rut is a dead end.

The bus drops me off a few blocks from my building. I run to the back door and work my way around the bins to the punch clock. The room is small and lined with cubbies. Mail arrives in banded bundles. I sort the envelopes into slots. I know every zip code in Clifton and Paterson. I imagine the envelopes are knives, each piercing a tiny bird trapped in a wooden box.

A rut is an inverted ritual.

I'm scribbling a poem in my notepad when my boss walks in. He asks if I've seen his new Porsche and invites me for a spin around the block. The phone rings and I answer it. *It's your wife,* I say. He rushes upstairs and I transfer the call. I flip back to my poem. The phone rings again. I transfer the call and flip back to my poem. The phone rings again. I transfer the call and flip back to my poem. The phone rings again. I transfer the call and flip back to my poem. The phone rings. Jesus Fucking Christ.

A rut is a saw.

I dial the number and read the pitch. Yes, says the man on the other end of the line. It's 3:00 AM, halfway through my night shift, and I nearly fall off my chair. This is my first Yes all week. I verify his address. Did you just say *Ar-kan-sas?* He laughs out loud. I repeat the address. He laughs again. *You mean Ar-kan-SAW?* he says. *Where in the heck you from?* I think about Dorothy. So it's *Kan-saw,* then?

A rut is tiny bluebirds nesting. Some mornings you imagine one might soar. None does. They're already tired. Routine devoured their wings. They lie still and whisper: leave.

Six bus tubs cover the floor and my counter is stacked with dishes. I pre-rinse each plate with the hose, then load the dishwasher. The spray valve has a single setting: monsoon. I'm soaked down to my bra. The machine maintains a 180 degree rinse water temperature, which means on exit the dishes are hot. I pull on gloves, stack the clean plates on the rack, then pull a tub off the floor, pre-rinse, and reload the washer. My friend Rosa walks in from the bar bearing gifts in the form of two Jager shots. We step into the cooler and shut the door. I wrap an arm around myself. My teeth chatter. *Let's stay here all night*, I whisper.

A rut is a cycle. You roam—replace one dead end with another.

It's 11:00 AM and I've been at it for four hours. I hang up the phone, push the button for Do Not Disturb and walk to the corner liquor store. The clerk waves me in and rings up the usual. I run back to the office, fill the ice trays with water and rush to my desk. Two voicemails. I dial the numbers and schedule appointments for upholstery and carpet cleaning. I update the board. An hour later my boss walks in, sparks a cigar, and pours his lunch into a glass. Out in the shop I hear the truck roll in. I pour half a bottle of wine into a red plastic cup and stand by the doorway smoking a cigarette. After the fourth pot of coffee, I ring the warehouse bell to signal the day's midpoint. Rituals help us through.

A rut is an open door with rusted hinges that swings both ways. Was the light on? Who was in the room? What was I wearing? The truth is blurred. Certainty is that thing we're after.

It's Monday morning. I check the voicemail, water the plants, order supplies for the week, make coffee, and organize the storage closet. Then I sit at my desk with a full mug and a calculator prioritizing bill payments for Friday's paycheck. A white bird flies onto the windowsill in the kitchen like a bad omen. I pour myself a second cup. The bird flaps its wings. My boss walks in and says *sorry, but I won't be able to pay you until the 25th.* The bird bangs its head against the glass.

A rut is drought.

A dog turd greets me at the door. In the kitchen—a bong on the counter, three-dozen beer cans and a sink full of dishes. It's 7:00 AM on a Sunday. I'd rather be in bed with the boyfriend, but it's 2008 and the economy's tanked. I need this hustle. I take out the trash, load the dishwasher, wipe down the counters, vacuum, mop, and spray the curtains with Febreze. I make the bed, pull the gun out from under the pillow using a hand towel and place it on the nightstand. Then I walk into the bathroom and holy fuck. I step out to the patio, lend myself a shot of tequila, and call the homeowner. *Sorry,* he answers. *I meant to warn you about that. We had a hell of a party Friday night and the Jacuzzi overflowed. A few of the girls drank too much and never made it to the toilet. Will an extra $50 cover it?*

A rut is a number.

Things my mother says: With any luck, we're gonna work 'til the day we die. *I have friends who could count them all on a single hand—the places they've lived, the people they've been, the jobs they've held. I've always envied this kind of stability. I've always feared this kind of stability. I've lived here and there, been this and that, worked everywhere. Another day, another dollar, so it goes.*

THE HEAD CLOWN

Sean Finucane Toner

> There's nothing funny about a clown in the moonlight.
> —attributed to Lon Chaney Sr.

I: THE STRAIGHT MAN

Back in the early '90s, just three doors down from the head clown's house, I moved words for minimum wage. It had seemed the perfect job for me, my acting as stock lad and clerk at a cozy bookstore on the South Jersey barrier island Ocean City.

When I unpacked and shelved the shipments of books, I moved through the collections of Poe and Hawthorne who had been my childhood bedtime storytellers. Past Frank Herbert and Arthur C. Clark, who had guided me through the troubles of my early teens, and past Goethe who had inspired me to aim far beyond my reach.

I spent my summer days among old friends and entertained fantasies that the bespectacled girl of my dreams would pull *The Fountainhead* off the shelf, and we'd engage in an intimate conversation about the evil queen of literature. We'd hit it off and spend our summer on the beach, or in a park beneath a bough, feeding each other grapes and arousing each other with passages from *Atlas Shrugged*. Just out of college, I had an excuse.

Sadly, my Khayyam-esque daydreams weren't going to materialize at Barrier Books. Too naive to realize that certain inferences would be drawn about *me* from my surroundings, I stocked books and music, I worked the register, made stationery deliveries, and on occasion, colorfully coiffed my answers to a certain Manhattan bestseller list. "Yes. One hundred and seventy-six copies of *Faust*. Is this going on all over the country?" I waited a minute and said, "Just teasing."

The store also sold music: Classics, Jazz, Broadway. Everything from Bernadette Peters singing in *Mack and Mabel* to *Cats* in English, *Cats* in Japanese, *Cats* in German:

> Eine Katze so klug wie magische Mr. Mistoffelees!
> Oh! Nun, ich nie! Gab es jemals

Craig, the proprietor, who a screenplay might describe as a "friendly bachelor uncle" himself wore maroon polo shirts with the *Barrier Books and Music* imprimatur embossed upon them. A black-and-white stage shot of Craig standing over a seated Talulah Bankhead hung over the tape deck. The picture hinted at Craig having had a much richer, earlier life than the cozy, book-selling one on Barrier Island.

His partner, Ricky, wasn't quite so genteel as Craig. His choreographed fashions and his obsession with haute couture didn't put him in the same circles as his senior companion. Much of Ricky's time before and after work was spent at the mile of undeveloped dunes and trails at the south end of the island, and his focus, during work, seemed to be on dispatching his spud duties quickly and efficiently, and then chronicling the sexual exploits of many of the customers.

We were three stereotypes in a resort island store—the genial bachelor uncle, his more flamboyant young ward, and a nerdly hetero who could not catch a romantic break. The bespectacled girl of my dreams would need powerful lenses to discern my orientation there in the middle of the Ziegfeld Follies.

One of several events pushed me into the dark, lonely, dirty, aggressively capitalist, predatory, nefarious, and horn-tooting profession of clowndom. Heavy parcels of Mylar balloons would come to the store every week or so. We'd pay COD from an envelope in the register, and a man I'll call Butch showed to retrieve the balloons. His real name I'll keep in reserve because the Clown and Mime Local 42 has been known to flatten a bulbous nose or two.

Butch, perpetually tan, shrewd-eyed, resembled an amiable version of one of Durer's devils. Every visit, he'd say something like, "How would you like to make some good money?"

I'd hem and haw and finally manage a "no." I fought myself from asking "How much?" I knew that clown paint, once applied, didn't wash off one's soul so easily. I did not want to become a boardwalk clown.

But he must have sniffed out my scent of Eau de Loser. Soon, he added things like, "There's a lot of attractive young women up on the boardwalk at night."

It didn't take this sales pitch long, though I can't remember exactly when I leased my soul to the head clown.

It might have been when a special order of *The Autobiography of Alice B. Toklas* came for a customer—my age—named Marianne. Ricky asked, "Want to run up to the department store and drop this off?"

"Do we usually make book deliveries?"

"You'll think she's cute," he said. "Maybe you can use some of your Irish charm on her." The way he said "charm" seemed to put quotes around it.

I made my way through the labyrinthian department store and to the returns department, stood in line with Gertrude Stein, edged forward as toasters and espadrilles were returned.

When the station neighboring Marianne's opened, I allowed the customer behind me to go, and a glance from Marianne told me she caught this. When my turn came, I went up to her station, nervously handed her the book, and told her that it had come.

She thanked me. She did not wear glasses, but was quite pleasing to my eye. "I'll have to pay at the store, though."

"That's all right."

We stood. I blinked. She stared.

Finally she said, "Is there anything else?"

Some moments of sexual tension, so delicious and so fleeting, were meant to be savored. Others, like this, required a quick feint of Irish wit to turn things around.

One Mississippi. Two Mississippi. Three Mississippi. I shook my head and said, "No."

Not quite a clown yet. But definitely a fool.

Then there was the Rita Mae Brown delivery. Ricky dispatched me to a lagoon house in the Gardens section of the island. I parked at the curb of the pink edifice. After walking past the similarly pinked golf cart, I knocked on the door. "Is Susie here?" I asked the senior woman who I had seen wheeling the cart around town all my summers.

"She's around back in the lagoon," the Pink Queen told me.

As I headed around back, the vision of a lounge chair and a bottle of suntan lotion danced in my head. When I reached the lagoon side of the house, though, I found nobody. "Susie?" I called, as if to an old friend.

"Down here."

When I reached the bulwark, I looked down, found a buff, tan, and very platinum young woman. Susie appeared a more taut version of Susan Powder, the diet guru and radical feminist.

But still.

"Who are you?" she said from her lavender kayak at the bottom of the ladder.

"I'm Sean Toner," I responded, as if she were taking careful note for that night's diary entry. "Ricky sent me with the book you ordered."

"A home delivery? Works for me."

Again, because quick repartee between the sexes only existed in plays and movies for me, and because I wasn't familiar with all the terrain on the orientation map, I stood, uncertain.

"Could you leave it on the table behind you?" she said, followed by, "Tell Ricky I'll come by with the cash."

I nodded and made a hasty retreat. But at the table, I slipped *Rubyfruit Jungle* out of its brown paper bag and read the back cover. My shoulders drooped, my lungs deflated, and though I wasn't a clown yet, I was more than a fool. I was a straight man. Or at least an aspiring one.

My donning of the frilly pajamas didn't take place much after my most embarrassing Barrier Books moment. Ricky called after I had gone home one afternoon, said, "Someone came in today that you might be interested in."

"Am I going to have to deliver a book to her?"

He went on to describe her attractive neighbor-girl looks, her love of books, her being enrolled at one of the then Seven Sisters. "And she put in an application to work."

Ignoring the store's small size and that it probably already had one employee more than needed, I spent the night fantasizing. I pictured the two of us bumping into each other in the Sci Fi section. I imagined Hepburn-Tracey style arguments over placement of Natalie Cole and Frank Sinatra. I dreamed up long lunches at a nearby restaurant called Say Cheese.

The next day I crossed several lines, took her name and address from her application, and wrote one of my own to her. I gave my name and address, then filled in the 'desire position' section with "Friend, maybe more," before starting over without those last two words. For references, I listed Lord Byron, William Butler Yeats, and Hector Berlioz. I doubted that any of them were at liberty to answer questions about me, but I had thought these three might suggest something about my interests, and my world view.

I mailed the application to her. The elusive Seven Sisters' student came into the store at the end of the week, after I'd gone home. When Ricky called, he told me that she had received my application, that she felt the alternative books section in the back should be expanded to include more lesbian writers, and that her mother had been taken with my attempt.

•

But my donning of the garish plumage of the North American Board-walk Clown (Buffoonis stripmallis) probably took place because of Gay Talese's visit to the shop.

He strode in, better coiffed and better sartorially equipped for a tennis match than I had been for my grandfather's funeral. The strands of his DNA were clearly woven back to the first paters of the Roman Kingdom. He was accompanied by a younger woman, clearly kin, who stood in place while the entire bookstore, and my gaze, moved around her. Talese signed copies of *Unto the Sons*. My furtive glances at the woman—his daughter or niece—went unnoticed, or more likely, sensed and ignored. I had as much a chance with her as my cat did ordering a filet mignon at Le Bec Fin.

When the Taleses left, Ricky felt compelled to offer his opinion of the situation. "Forget it, Sean. She's so out of your league they won't even let you in the ballpark."

But this battle of esteem attrition did not turn me the way Ricky expected. The next time Butch came in to collect his shipment of Mylar, bummed a cigarette from Ricky's pack, and asked me if I wanted to work the boards, I said "yes."

After he lighted his cigarette, Butch said, "Good. I think it'll work out well for you."

And before I could stop myself, I answered, "Has anyone ever told you that you look like the devil?"

II: BOARDWALK PAGLIACCI

From the hour I got home until zero hour, I watched the Weather Channel. But no green indicating cloud cover showed, much less the red patches that told of threatening thunderstorms. I had agreed to suit up and sell balloons, and neither God nor nature would offer me relief.

I set out to meet my fate.

When I arrived at La Chateau Butch I noticed, for the first time, that the panes of the ground floor windows were painted white. Curtains blew out of unscreened windows on the second and third floors, and a single solar panel sat atop its steep roof. As I started up the stairs, Butch called out from the open first floor door.

I peered in at a dark, unfinished, slightly cool room. Just inside the door and along one of the painted windows stood a phalanx of bronze tanks, shoulder-high, like a half-dozen torpedoes resting on their tails. Inflated balloons bobbed and jostled along the ceiling as Butch untangled their dangling strings. The Little Mermaid, the Happy Face, and the Mickey Mouse balloons bobbed and jostled as if they were in a mosh pit, expressing their own form of pent up, youthful energy.

He turned his head, said, "Your suit is on top of the dryer upstairs."

I merely nodded. I was as preoccupied by the bobbing Mylar as if I were still the five-year-old with the Snoopy lunch box.

While he unknotted the strings, he directed his gaze at the slightly deflated balloon at the end of the string he worked on. Once he had extricated its line, he pulled the balloon toward him, took it in his hands, and snuffed the air out of its tied end with a dramatic final gasp. I realized that the windows were painted to keep the ground floor at a relatively constant temperature—to minimize the need for balloon euthanasia.

I went up the creaking steps and through an open door, into a compressed, shabby home I'd call Victorian Vandal. I stood in an entryway smaller than most bathrooms, peered left into a living room set with dark wood furniture, a thin, color-sapped carpet, and two postwar items—a television and its remote. A skinny man with drapes of blond hair sat on the couch, hunched over the coffee table, and when I stepped into the room, I noticed he was eating Cheerios.

"Hey," I said.

"Hey."

We had made our introductory grunts, he went back to watching the Weather Channel, and I headed, instinctively, toward the back of the house. Two steps took me past the stairs up to the next floor, and then I stepped into the staging area. It was the cave where old porcelain slunk off to die. There was a washboard and basin, a pair of antique hospital bed stands, and a glass front cabinet out of a Norman Rockwell illustration.

At the back window were the washer and dryer, one white, one pea soup green—obviously not bought at the same yard sale. My attire lay crumpled on top of the dryer, and I lifted the flimsy pajama onesie. Left behind, a horn, a pair of big glasses *with* a bulbous red nose, and a canvas money pouch. *Just how dirty did this business get?*

Outside the house I stood in, three preteen children on a scruffy lawn huddled over something I couldn't see. A turtle? A dirty magazine? A man buried up to his head in the dirt? Behind them stood a two-story shack the color of an old boot. An attractive woman emerged from the backyard house, walked up to the kids, peered down at what they were doing, and spoke for a moment. Then she headed for the main house, past the back stairs, and around to the front.

Footsteps sounded behind me before she could have ascended, and I turned to find the cereal bowl guy lumbering through the staging area and into the adjoining kitchen. He was so tall and long-limbed that it seemed as if a golden sycamore uprooted itself to wash its breakfast bowl. At 6:00 P.M.

"Hey," he said as he passed me again.

"Hey," I answered, and the woman from the boot came in the door. She and the sycamore exchanged greetings, and then he took the stairs two at a time, then another set, and I heard keys working a lock.

The woman from the boot said, "You the new clown?"

I nodded, studied her face a moment too long, and said, "You look too happy for this gig."

"You'll learn how to fake it, too."

I smiled, a little, as she donned oversized plastic glasses.

•

After that, our coterie assembled in the tight living room. Eileen—the woman—in her pink polka dots, the sycamore in his faded green get up, me in my drab blue and yellow PJs, and Butch in red. Clearly, his need to stand out outweighed his concerns about his resemblance to a demon from *The Triumph of Death*. He handed out bundles of cash, told me "There's fifty. A ten. Four fives. Twenty ones. If you start to run low on ones, go buy a small drink from the nearest grill."

I nodded. Simple enough.

"Keep your pouch in front, your horn hooked over it. To protect your money. Keep your eyes open for teenage boys around you—they aren't there to buy balloons."

The sycamore stared at the TV intently, but his expression offered no clue about which he needed more: the night's pay, or for that band of green and red over Nebraska to magically materialize over the boardwalk.

Butch went on with the lesson. "We've got three sizes of balloons. There are the round ones. They go for three dollars. The odd shapes go for four. And the 'I Love You' balloon that has three parts—that one goes for five."

Eileen, across from me, seemed to focus all her attention on preventing her eyes from rolling.

"And how do I get these balloons into the hands of the balloon-buying public?" I asked.

"Honk your horn. Wave. Smile at the kids. You want their attention —not their parents."

A dark, sodden blanket of dread settled over me. I realized just what I had signed up for, and why the sycamore stared at the Weather Channel as if in prayer. "Should I give the kids lollipops and tell them I have more candy in my van?"

Eileen looked at me as if I had just voiced something that was written across all her time with Butch. She smiled.

Butch ignored me, said, "When someone asks you how much the balloons are, you tell them that different sizes are different prices. I've found that when there's a range in prices, buyers are more comfortable. They feel like they have choice. The question in their mind becomes which price, instead of why pay?"

Great, the Wharton Extension Program. Ever optimistic, I said, "What do I do when I run out?"

"Don't. When you start running low, come down to Eileen's station at Ninth Street and she'll give you a new supply. But don't get caught selling while you are walking. The city has rules about where we can operate—and you can't break the plane of the stores. You can't sell in the walking lanes."

"Who knew balloons could be such a serious business."

Nobody said anything. Eileen had stopped smiling. So I looked to my side, patted the couch, then lifted the cushion and looked under. I heaped on my performance, patted my shirt, pulled open each of my sleeves and peered in.

"What the hell are you doing?" the sycamore asked.

"There's four clowns in the room," I answered. "But I'm not seeing any *funny*."

•

Two fifty-pound boxes of deflated Mylar, four torpedo-sized helium tanks, a pair of handtrucks, the sycamore, me, and several dozen inflated balloons filled the back of Butch's van. I pushed the Mickey Mice and the Little Mermaids aside, and peered out the back windows at the apparent

141

cast of my night. Young tanned women with hair scrunchies headed away from the boardwalk as if they were the wake of all my hopes. Moving in our direction were sun-reddened families; mothers herding, children straggling fathers.

We stopped at the Eighth Street ramp and the sycamore and I helped Butch lug crates, a box of balloons, and a helium tank while Eileen waited. Once we had set up, I asked Butch where my post was going to be, and he uttered the grim one-word answer as if it were a death sentence: "Funtown."

III: MRS. PEANUT

Butch dropped Eileen and me, two tanks and a box of balloons on the boardwalk at Ninth Street—the axis of the island. Eileen and I chatted for a few moments, I probed her about her relationship with Butch, and I soon learned more than I was comfortable knowing. Eileen quickly let me know that our chatter interfered with the progress of business, and I started down my gauntlet of shame.

While Eileen honked and waved and smiled to draw attention, I soon discovered that my mere red-haired presence brought the focus of children and childish alike. Kids gawked and pulled on their parents' shirt hems, and young women working various grills gave me sideward glances. I could handle all that. More troublesome were the calls of the free-range clowns' natural predators—teenage boys.

They'd ask, "Couldn't get a real job?"

The next one would say, "Look, it's Homey D. Clown."

And the most frequent, "Homey don't play that." These last two were catch phrases from *In Living Color*, a Fox TV show of the early nineties whence Rosie Perez, J-Lo, and Jim Carey got their starts.

Halfway to my designated post, I caught a glimpse of a human-sized peanut standing at the threshold of one of the shops. I spotted the top hat, the black cane, the monocle. From a distance, it appeared Mr. Peanut had been enlisted to garner attention for one of the stores.

As I neared, I was blocked by kids asking about my balloons and fathers irritated with the answers. I told all that I could only sell at Funtown, my prearranged site. Once moving again, I scanned a block ahead for Funtown, and hadn't thought of Mr. Peanut until I had nearly reached him.

Mr. Peanut, I learned, had lithe arms and very shapely legs in tight leggings. Mr. Peanut was a Mrs. We made eye contact—me through my big glasses, her through her eyeholes. Someone clearly had self-esteem issues greater than mine. And I would never be comfortable around ballpark vendors again: "Peanuts. Get your peanuts here . . ."

I forged ahead, took up position at Funtown. Behind me, two dozen video games and their indigenous population of teenage boys. Further back—a half block of rides for young children. And right on the border between Funtown and the boardwalk, me, a marginally invested clown working out the plot of the novel that would win me an agent a year later. If I had known, I might have spent my time more wisely.

Instead, I honked, I untangled lines, I weathered the gusts of "Homey don't play that," and "Where's your sock, Homey?" This last was a reference to Homey D. Clown's weapon of choice, a sock with a tennis ball inside.

When the first families came to me, I gave them the scripted spiel about different sizes being different prices. From the start, though, the eye rolls and disgusted looks forced me to adapt my pitch to something different: "Do you want the LX, the DX, or the SX model?" But half my buyers needed explanation. Finally, I settled on, "I'm supposed to tell you that they are three different prices." This admittance of the business behind the balloons made nearly everybody—including myself—feel better. Every once in a while, though, I'd run into a humorless father or a macho boyfriend who'd react as if I were knocking down the fourth wall—and the plaster hit them in the head. Shabby as it was, I had a role to play.

Early, I learned that a moving clown drew more attention than a standing one. When I set off toward Eileen for restocking, the kids would come with their parents in tow. At first I responded to their "Hey Mr. Clown, are the balloons free?" and the "How much are they?" with the proper, "I have to get out of traffic." Then I started selling in the off-limits zone. Then I figured out I'd draw even more buyers if I moved against the flow of traffic, very very slowly.

Eileen began to wonder how I kept needing reloads so quickly.

"It's how I toot my horn," I said.

Though I'd learned to saunter through the evening crowds, I tried to draw anybody gathered around me past Mrs. Peanut. When I passed her alone, I would give a quick honk, and eventually, she'd tap the cane on the boardwalk. But this call-and-response was as far as I'd break through her shell.

Then I'd be back at the front of the dreaded Funtown, listening to the flurry of sounds of the video games behind me.

"Homey don't play that!"

One night, two enterprising high schoolers pulled a water pistol drive-by. After they sprayed me, they walked away, laughing.

Though my wounds were not grievous, the assault to my dignity was serious enough that these little bastards were going to feel the wrath of clown. I wiped the pistol spit from my face, gathered myself, and gave them just a little lead time. Then I pursued them through the ever-thickening crowds. The pair were tipped off as I neared—either they caught the children pulling on their parent's sleeves, or they saw that many of the eyes ahead of them were aimed just behind them, or they heard the hollow fump-fump of the balloons jostling against each other. I wove the strings between my outer fingers and then had my hands up just as the boys looked behind them. I clamped my claws around their necks, and spoke in a low voice. "Now you've got my attention."

Even though those guys could have decked me, they were all scrunched and scared with my bookworm grip on their necks.

I said, "So, what are we going to do together? Go play some pool at Jilly's? Get some pizza? Maybe I can help you pick up chicks."

The boy on the right tried to wriggle away, but I firmed my grip and whispered, "Homey don't play that." There was something very liberating, and empowering, about playing a mad clown. Neither Leoncavallo nor Stephen King would have it any other way.

When I finally let go, my hand went down to the horn and I walked with them ten more steps, honking away. Ee-er. Ee-er. Ee-er. They ran off, I waited for them to turn and come to their senses, but they didn't. Then I went back to Funtown.

The next day or so the Barrier Island apparatchik, in his short-sleeve button-down and blue tie, walked up. As if he were Patton demanding to speak to my commanding officer, he said, "Where's your boss?"

"The head clown?" I asked. "He's down at Eighth Street."

The bureaucrat marched off, leaving me dimly aware that this might concern me. I waited a full fifteen before I strolled through the crowd for a resupply.

IV: A CARNIVAL EVENING

The next time I clowned, I was "promoted." That's how Butch described it when he dropped me off at Eighth Street with the helium tanks and the box of balloons. He stationed me catty-corner to the Music Pier, between an upscale clothing store and a grill.

It didn't take long for me to scratch away at this lottery ticket: I could no longer make myself conspicuous on the boards. But now I was conspicuous to an attractive young woman who worked the grill. She didn't wear glasses—but she was close to Jodie Foster in appearance and voice.

I broke a lot of twenties—and tens, and fives—for change while I was at my new post. But when the grill girl told me her name was Charli, the gender shuffle of my summer forced me to steal a quick glance at her throat. "That's short for Charlene," she answered my expression.

The short jaunt to her counter didn't offer me much chance to market myself. So, several times a night I'd find it necessary to make for the water fountains a block away, or head for the men's room in the Music Pier. Then I got the idea to ask Charli for her grill number, then made the slow walk to the pay phones. Several times a night I'd call her, place a soda-and-hot-dog order, then feign reluctance when approached by eager kids.

It didn't take long for Charli to start breaking my stones. "You're allowed to order at the counter like everyone else."

"I like to call my favorite grill every once in a while," I said. I think we both knew that these regular calls were a combination of marketing strategy and strange flirtation.

At the end of one night, when the crowds had thinned and I could hear the waves breaking on the beach, Charli came up and bought a balloon. I hadn't yet worked up the nerve, to ask her out but my eating habits must have given her a clue.

When she told me, "It's for my daughter," she must have caught the dismay on my face. She said, "My ex has her now."

We chatted for a few minutes before she asked, "How come you haven't asked me out yet?"

I opened my arms, looked down over my outfit.

"At least I know what I'd be getting," she said.

This moment answered a summer of longing and bode well for my dreams as a writer; Charli had read through the big glasses, the tangle of red hair, the obnoxious tooting—and found something worth looking into further.

"You working tomorrow night?" she asked.

"If I'm lucky."

Soon, the van pulled up behind me, and Butch and the sycamore started carting the tanks and balloons down. I followed, climbed into the van, Charli's number written on a receipt. In a different time, we'd have piled on the back of a wagon. We'd have been a troupe of minstrels, or troubadours, or jugglers.

I would later learn that Butch had been an Army drill sergeant, that he dated an opera singer, that he played monthly poker with a poet of national significance.

What impressed me most, though, was a night late in the summer of my clowning. I had been up at an amusement pier with Charli and she was keen on the rides that pressed our bodies against each other's: the Scrambler, the Salt-n-Pepper Shakers, the Tilt-a-Whirl. When, later, she stopped into the restrooms at the Music Pier, I stood across the boardwalk and down a dozen yards from Butch. I observed how easy he was with the customers, how comfortable he was talking with kids in a way that was neither condescending nor creepy. I reminded myself to ask him how long he'd been working the boards, how long he'd had to weather disdain from select fathers and taunts from acne-ridden critics.

Now, that summer with Charli is gone, Barrier Books is gone, my Royal Manual is gone. It is as if the boardwalk and the island have vanished. Life has become an accumulation of disappearances. How much more could I offer, as a writer, than something colorful and buoyant. Could I do any better than write words that rose defiant, against gravity?

BEYOND WORDS, WORLDS, AND PAMPERS

Roisin McLean

If this essay were a movie, we would view a leisurely pan of constellations on night sky, leap into the sparkling void, and turn toward the orb of the earth, dabbed with regional clouds above the United States, and zoom in at such speed we would be flung into the past—all the way back to the 1960s in Lionville, PA, and a housing development amidst farms where horse manure, spread as fertilizer on the field up the hill, spiced the summer air around childhood play and wafted

through a window in a split-level house to a girl lying on her bed reading until the sun went down. By age ten, I had become an avid reader—I loved Edgar Rice Burroughs and the aroma of Dover Publications' paper and binding, which masked the fertilizer stench when I held the book close to my face (a must for nearsighted eyes)—discovered *The Secret Garden* and *Jane Eyre*, and wondered if I could ever transport people to other worlds through writing.

A few years later, at Downingtown High School, I wrote my first short story as a response to a choice of picture prompts. Immersing myself in a centuries-old woodcut print of people committed to an asylum, I wrote in first person about patients suffering in agony from various mental and physical disabilities, torturous delusions, wrongful incarceration, and the cruelty of our caretakers. The woodcut was minimalist but suggestive, and a plethora of details surged to mind. Fifty years later, although my handwritten-in-cursive story has disappeared with the lint of time, I can still recall the last line: "And that's how I got here, St. Peter." (Which I

148

thought very clever.) A few days after the assignment was due, the teacher announced that one of the stories was exceptional, and she would read it aloud to the class. I loved that teacher, Miss Fletcher.

We switch from film media to still photos here. Note the prim, proper, and pleasing image of Miss Fletcher, with her 1950s pageboy hairdo, cardigan, crisp white blouse, below-the-knee wool skirt, and brown loafers with shiny Lincoln pennies and leather fringe. She was by nature calm, gentle, and encouraging, and she endeared herself to me further by reading my story to the class, which crystallized my dream of writing.

When I was 16, *The Philadelphia Bulletin*, Sunday Magazine section, published my first poem for 1 cent per line. Sixteen cents! Naturally, I anticipated writing the great American novel by age 25. But it took decades for me to perceive the last line of my first short story as more of a cop-out than a clever, fully realized O. Henry ending, for example. So what happened? Life. The life I needed to experience in order to write with credibility, even if the genre were fantasy.

Return to movie mode here and fast forward past many stories, written for the English Department at Penn State, some of which I still have on onion skin paper with fading ink from my first two-tone blue Royal typewriter. (I should mention that was *after* I tried and failed miserably at majoring in pre-veterinary medicine, which more than one girl did who loved dogs and never got a horse for her birthday.) I double-majored in English—the Language and Literature program and the Writing and Editing program—and graduated with a B.A. and a full half of my college credits in those programs. College curricula are rarely structured that way today, so I was fortunate.

Zoom into the future and freeze frame on the publishing company, Prentice-Hall, Inc., NJ, where I landed my first job with help from my Uncle Ed—as a production editor in the College Division, starting in the proofreading pool. Little did I know that my great fortune at finding employment only a month after college graduation typecast me like an actor—and it eventually felt more like a double brand with a cattle iron—because I started (1) in college textbooks, and (2) on "hard side," the jargon for engineering and technical texts. I might as well have been blacklisted; no publisher would consider me for a position in Trade Books, which is where I wanted to be, or even on the "soft side" (English and liberal arts texts) of a College Division. Pleased to have a job at all, however, as well as one dealing with the written word (even if it was $e = mc^2$), I became a workaholic and worked my way up the ladder to Supervisory Editor and then (new freeze frame) across the Hudson River to the Big Apple and Managing Editor at Macmillan Publishing Company—at 53rd and Third, around the corner from the slant-roofed Citicorp building and nine blocks northwest of the United Nations. To my mid-30s mind, I had "arrived."

Zoom into the future again to marriage and pregnancy, when I quit in-house staff work to stay home and raise my daughter—the joy of my life, then, now, and always. While she slept (and she was fairly catatonic for her first 18 months), I started a freelance book production business, which lasted 10 years, actually a quarter century given the on-again/off-again nature of the freelance market. The upshot? I read no books (except for *Goodnight Moon* and the like, aloud for my daughter) and wrote no fiction in all those years. Sad but true—as a workaholic who read and edited for 60 hours per week, I sought anything other than reading or writing as entertainment. And one day, while copyediting for a university press an arcane manuscript on Dutch shipping in the 1600s, I cried out, fearful my brain would implode, "UNCLE, please save me from myself." Editing, so close to writing, was not nearly close enough to the writing I wanted to do, and I needed a reason for being in addition to motherhood.

That would be the corner between a rock and a hard place, and I knew something must change. Instead of trying to change my profession, I recorded (between Pamper changes, naps, and editing) the visual images of my soundless meditations over a 5-year period. Revisions and thematic reorganization of the originally chronological meditations brought me great pleasure, and I titled the resulting chronicle, *Beyond Words: Journey of the Spirit, Spirit of the Journey.* After that labor of love, I sought feedback at church from my trusted spiritual advisor, who was dubbed Elkdreamer by a Native American holy man he mysteriously met in a remote cave hours into some New Mexico desert (I suspect peyote was involved). Elkdreamer read my chronicle and to my utter delight described it as "Lewis Carroll and Castaneda with a pinch of Vonnegut for seasoning." Confidence led me to imagine fictionalizing the piece, whose characters (Woman, White Horse, Lion, and Jester) are reminiscent of those in *The Wizard of Oz*, and the result could have great potential as an intergenerational novel. To my dismay, writer's block slammed me with horrific force, and I could conceive of myself as nothing more than a mother with wannabe writer ambitions. Which sounds horrendously negative—on the bright side, mothering my precious daughter provided a continuum of joy throughout the years and, not that I understood it at the time, intriguing plots for stories to come.

The film theme permits us to skip about two decades by doing just that, skipping them entirely, and bringing into focus me still stifled in my writing and bored by empty days with my daughter away at college. I gave up writing and interpreted my silent meditations as a literal sign. Still quasi-editing for a living, I entered a part-time Interpreter for the Deaf Program at Union County College. After 2 years of learning and loving American Sign Language (ASL), it became clear that my strong command of and love for the English language blocked my ability to interpret into sign, because I could think only in English, not in sign. Consequently, I transferred from the interpreting program to the ASL and Deaf Studies program and earned a certificate. I still enjoy the challenge of "translating" (more precisely, linguistically "glossing") English poetry into ASL poetry in which rhyme appears as signs with similar hand shapes, for example, making rhyme repetition visual.

During the ASL time frame, I also took a part-time course in C-Print® captioning, which combines software that converts phonetic code into English, fast typing on a laptop, and a captionist's summarizing skills of a speaker's meaning (a form of writing that demanded simultaneous use of both hemispheres of the brain, and which, I told myself, would hone my writing and revising skills). Learning on the job—yes, I finally could change my profession—I provided real-time captioning and study-note transcripts for hard-of-hearing students in the classroom (middle school, high school, and college). I always felt badly that it took me 3 years to gain proficiency, yet the work paid well, and I thrived on the fulfillment engendered by grateful students. After 8 years, I wearied of typing other people's words. After another 4 years, my then student graduated, and I found myself jobless after 40 years of employment, with skills suddenly far too specialized for the employment market. As with other baby boomers, the 180° flip-flop in the professional-specialization trend booted me out into the cold. I had to resort to unemployment, which at the time I considered shameful but for which I will always be thankful.

The movie here paces itself with alternating glimpses of multiple events that overlap in time. First, I wanted to type my own words and decided to return to my roots, so to speak. To help me realize the dream, I entered the low-residency MFA program in Creative Writing at Fairleigh Dickinson University. I cannot rave enough about the praiseworthy caliber and feedback of the mentors, all published authors, the program's social dynamics with mentors and fellow students and the community we formed, and the instilled discipline of writing and revising. Within a few years, I published my first short story and then another and another, all without financial remuneration, which did not dampen my joy.

Second, to keep food on the table after my divorce, I took a part-time position with a college as a writing tutor, which helped appreciative students with their writing as much as I gained from the experience and could bring to my own writing. Unfortunately, although the college required its tutors to have or be working toward an MFA or Master's degree, the hourly rate of only $16 (WTF?) resulted in, surprise surprise, not enough food on the table.

Third, I considered becoming an adjunct professor at the college but rejected the idea because I could not think quickly on my feet. For example, if asked, "Who wrote *The Scarlet Letter*?" I'd probably respond: "Nathaniel Hawthorne. No, he wrote *Silas Marner*, so it must have been Erich Fromm. No, he wrote *Freshman English*. Or was the title, *It All Started with Freshman English*? No, that was a different author, George Eliot, I think—the one who wrote *The Art of Loving*. Or was it Ethan Frome? Or Edith Wharton? What was the question?"

Fourth, somewhere in those years I earned a Certificate of Eligibility, High School Teacher of English, which fell by the wayside with the idea of adjunct professorship.

Fifth, the unemployment agency introduced me to the Workforce Investment Act (WIA), which paid for a 5-month course in web design.

I enjoyed the work, but the software bugs made me nuts, which would be bearable, I determined, if I created websites only for authors. Two websites and 5 years later ….

Alas, even though I could wear numerous "different hats," what with my skills in writing, editing, book production, teaching, tutoring, web design, and captioning—all of which revolve around the hub called *word*—I felt stymied every which way I turned. The film here summarizes in CGI an animated word cloud artwork in the shape of a wheel, with *word* at the hub, my skills as the spokes, and a broken rim—the wheel turns only so far before thudding to a halt.

I never expected to celebrate turning 62, but thank goodness for early retirement and 40 years of paying into Social Security. The film here alternates images of fireworks, champagne corks popping, smiling people giving each other "high fives," mortar boards flung high into the air. Retirement—time to write! Right? Writer's block slammed me again for 3 years, during which time I discovered that one cannot survive on Social Security. The movie flips briefly to interspersed frames of Homer Simpson spurting "Doh" and me babbling "Duh"!

Having downsized to a condo, I discovered I must move yet again, this time to a state with lower property taxes. A wise man once told me, "When you have way too much to do, that's when to write." And so, now officially a senior citizen on Medicare—and in the midst of packing, moving, unpacking, remodeling residences, packing again to move again, and existential and aging crises (the film illustrates these events in fast motion although they felt intolerably slow)—I finished revising my collection, *The Fifth Eye*, and published it with a top-notch independent publishing house. I finally feel like a writer, an author, because I am one. I always was, but I kept getting in my own way and allowing self-sabotage, which I had perceived as fate, to throw me off course at countless junctures.

With that lesson learned, the film segues into a slow pan of rosy gold and magenta clouds tinting sky over evergreen trees on the bank of a river in early evening and reflecting like an impressionistic painting on the rippling waves. What lies over that treed horizon? After I settle in a new state, near my daughter and her hubby, I will write for their precious newborn, Adelaide Eve, a fictionalized version of my compiled soundless meditations in *Beyond Words*, penned about 22 years ago. Taking a tip from L. Frank Baum, I could fashion myself as a Dorothy, but perhaps with different personae, such as Glinda the Good Witch and her flip side, the Wicked Witch of the West. Other characters could (and do) simulate the Scarecrow (Jester), the Cowardly Lion (Lion), and the Tin Man (White Horse). As for the man behind the curtain, I do not consider the Wizard a humbug from Omaha, and I will probably veer from Baum's plot and ending, but maybe I will not, because *Beyond Words* includes a Trickster (Jungian-archetype style). In any case, who will my wizard be? And how might I portray the Winged Monkeys as good rather than evil, à la the Broadway musical *Wicked*? Ooh, so many questions and possibilities inviting words onto the page. Perhaps the writing process and its addicting, titillating sparks of creation will provide the clues for my next book. ("My next book"—how savory those words taste on the tongue.) I look forward to discovering the story (amid hot flashes and grandchild Pamper changes) with all the rapture a writer can conceive, which is vast given the myriad splendid moments in life that we all have lived, in one way or another.

HANDLING ANOTHER MAN'S WOMAN (With or Without Permission)

Thomas E. Kennedy

At a New York City party in the 1990s, a guest asked my daughter what language you speak in Denmark.

"Danish," Isabel replied.

"But...but..."The girl was confused; apparently, she was not the brightest of lights. "Danish is something you eat!"

When I arrived in Denmark in 1972, everyone in Copenhagen spoke some English, often proficiently. It was part of the charm of this city. But I quickly learned that the Danes prefer to speak Danish among themselves, and you can feel out of place in a Danish party or dinner if you can't speak the language. In Denmark, most Danes presume that you speak Danish or will learn to speak it if you are more than a couple of months in the country. The Danes will carry you for a while, but they soon abandon you—as I discovered at a wedding party with my Danish girlfriend where I soon found myself sitting on a staircase, alone; fellow guests came over to me and spoke a few English sentences, but they drifted away when their hospitable duty was done.

Before I learned Danish—some Danes would say I never learned—I used to translate newspaper articles from *Politiken* and *Information* and the occasional poem into English to see how they made sense. Although my accent is atrocious, I quickly became good at it, and Danish writers and poets gravitated toward me for a voice in the English-speaking world, the big world. After all, the Danish language is spoken by only about 5.4 million people—approximately 5/9ths the population of the state of New Jersey.

The lingua franca of most Europeans internationally is English. It is the new Latin. The Dutch, Portuguese, all the Nordic people, the Central and East Europeans, the Germans, Italians, and even the French and the Spanish have given over to it. That is, they speak their native tongue at home, but they speak English when with tourists and when they're in another country—"American," as the Danes call it, because America is where the money is, the perception of money. The wide chrome bumpers that used to be on American cars, Danes call "a dollar grin."

Within ten years I was publishing in literary journals my English translations of poems—"American," I had to stipulate in my grant proposals to the Danish Arts Council. In 1976, an editor who hired me for a Danish magazine published in English made me swear to use British-English rather than American. "Americans do not speak English!" he said. The board member who was championing me for the job commented, "Yes, why adjust to the greater world when you can adapt to a smaller one."

The markets for poetry were mostly non-paying ones, the American literary journals. *Name me one poet who earns any money?* Colonel Cathcart announces in *Catch-22* and ex-PFC Wintergreen responds, T. S. Eliot! Eliot notwithstanding, most American poets earn their money from subsidiary activities. But most translators earn money; not a lot, but some. I am dumb-founded to explain to my Danish poet friends why I make a thousand or two thousand dollars on Danish State grants from translating their poems while they earn nothing. However, they are content to get out in the English-speaking (American) world with sights on aesthetic values of getting out in the larger world—and perhaps some ultimate, pecuniary reward; it never comes—except, in the rare cases, from subsidiary activities in the U.S.

However, Danish poets receive money from the number of books they have on public library shelves (*Bibliotek penge*) and from State grants —there is a tidy one-year grant, a three-year one, even a life-time grant —and, if the poets are extraordinarily fortunate, Nordic money, from the Nordic Literary Prize. Danes expect to be paid for their work, including poetry. Translation into English is a sort of fancy dressing on the salad.

It is all in the interest of preserving the language, so it does not become a "vulnerable language" and eventually die. Moreover, Danes are happy with what poets bring to their language, even if they do not read poetry other than in school or the daily or weekly poem in some newspapers.

I read a comment by some poet—I think it was Rumi—that entrusting your poem to a translator was like permitting another man to handle your woman. "Sexist!" you might shout, although in this Post-truth Age of Donald, one might excuse that as mere celebrity locker-room talk: *Grab her by the metaphor.*

The first Danish poems I translated into English were, in fact, by a woman—so what would that lady say, Entrusting your poem to a translator is like permitting another man to handle your man? I continued to translate Pia Tafdrup for ten or fifteen years, mesmerized by her poems —and Pia claimed that I had won her a 1994 contest, when she was less well-known, due to an interview with her that I had published in the Danish cultural newspaper, *Weekendavisen*—until I admitted that David McDuff did it better. McDuff translates from the Russian as well as the Danish, and while I was versed in Dostoevsky (in Constance Garnett translations, a woman who was handling a man's prose!), Pia had some arcane Russian influence to her poetry that eluded me, as evidenced by her collection *Tarkskovij's Horses.* I had to admit that McDuff rendered into English Tafdrup's poetry better than I ever could—a notch above my translations. That was a hard-won admission for me, but I was a better person for it.

You see, in my soon six decades as a writer, the first two I passed not getting published (I had a big-time agent, lots of encouragement from teachers and editors, but no acceptances, until 1981). For the last forty years, I have published mainly prose—a score of poems that (since I'm admitting things) were not very good (they had come to me of a piece; I could not revise, lest I break the spell), alongside some forty books of prose and hundreds of stories and essays. Good poetry is the sublime height of language; some reviewers accused me of having some lyrical passages in my prose, but not one book of poetry. (Iben Andersen, a dishy and proficient, award-winning young Danish book binder, "published" a book of my verse in stylish hardback—in two or three copies, one for me, one for Iben—but I put the "published" in quotation marks, a beautiful but nugatory publication.)

I am blocked from writing poetry. I cannot figure out where lines should end, or how one should begin a poem or how it ends. I always ended after the ending or began before the beginning. But when I translated poems, all those problems were solved. Translating poems, I felt like a poet, felt instrumental to the poem, felt I was singing.

On Danish Radio (DR) in 2008 being interviewed about an anthology of *New Danish Writing* which I had guest-edited for *The Literary Review* (then under the editorship of Walter Cummins), I was talking about some poems I had translated by Janus Kodal, Jørgen Leth, Martin Glaz Serup, Maja Lucas, Dy Plambeck, and ten poems of Henrik Nordbrandt. Nordbrandt had been the inspiration for the 200-page anthology.

The way it happened: I had been in Kastrup Airport, about to fly to New York, when I picked up an issue of *Den Blå Port* (which I translated as *The Blue Port*, rather than *The Blue Gate*, for reasons described in the introduction of the anthology). There were six poems by Henrik Nordbrandt in that issue of *Den Blå Port*; on the plane, I turned to them first. I was astonished. I thought, I must translate these. And I did so, racing in a metal tube through the sky over the Atlantic, in handwriting, directly on the margins of the journal pages, English alongside the printed Danish, complete with air pocket zig-zags of my MontBlanc. When I got to Fairleigh Dickinson University in New Jersey where I would be teaching, I found that I was sharing a dormitory suite with the then poetry editor of Emerson College's *Ploughshares*, David Daniel, himself a formidable poet and friend. Late one evening in our living room over vodka, I did a reading of my Nordbrandt translations for him. When I was done, David stared at me in silence. Then he asked, "Would you read them again?"

I read them aloud twice more, thinking perhaps the vodka had prevented me from enunciating sufficiently. When I finished reading the last translation, David said, "Those are completely fucking awesome!"

Which encouraged me to type up my translations, with funds from the Danish Arts Council, and send them to *The New Yorker* and *American Poetry Review*. Such submissions are always accompanied by a strong measure of fatalism—what's the use? But try anyway. After all, the verb "submit" means that one is subjugating the writing to the judgment of an editor; in the case of *The New Yorker*, one is subjugating by email to the "Poetry Editor," not a name, merely a generic person—who knows what person will respond to it, or not. Within a few days, Alice Quinn, then poetry editor of *The New Yorker*, emailed, thanking me warmly for introducing her to Nordbrandt's work, singling out the ones she most admired, although the magazine was overstocked and would not be publishing any of these six. Okay, a rejection, but a rave rejection: From Alice Quinn! From *The New Yorker*! Better still, *American Poetry Review* wrote back, accepting five of the six; they appeared in the March-April 2008 issue (at one dollar a line in addition to the $1,500 I'd received from a grant).

I told this story to the DR interviewer—in Danish, with my atrocious accent—and next day, I was telephoned by one Barry Lereng Wilmont, an artist and publisher and translator to Danish, who told me that if I could translate Henrik Nordbrandt, I could translate Dan Turèll.

"Yeah, but," I said—Turèll was one of the most celebrated poets and writers in Denmark, dead at the age of 47—"Dan Turèll is already translated."

"No."

Dan had loved all things American. He felt an affinity to America, but he was not translated and published there. Dan died in 1993, fifteen years before my phone conversation with Barry Lereng Wilmont. Dan always wanted to be translated into American. He expected that his friend and colleague Barry could; born in Manitoba, Canada, Barry was brought at four by his Danish mother in 1940. When the Germans invaded Denmark that April, he was secreted in Jutland, and he lived his life here, learning Danish over his mother tongue, went to the Royal Academy in his twenties to become an artist and medalist. Barry could translate into Danish from English. He had translated T. S. Eliot, Paul Celan, Ezra Pound, but he could not translate Turèll to American.

Barry was charged by Dan to secure the translation into American and publication in the U.S. of his work. Turèll was a cult figure, had a café and a Square named after him and a literary Society set up and published a hundred books in his short lifetime. Barry had taken fifteen years, since Dan's death, to find a translator, possibly he had found one in me.

He told me all these things over beers in Jeppes Badehotel—Jeppe's Baths Hotel, which has neither a spa nor a hotel nor a Jeppe, but it was an artist hang-out—a brown bar in Nyhavn, a former prostitutes' and sailors' quarter that has been gentrified.

Although I settled in Copenhagen in 1976—began frequenting it in '72—as, I guess I must say, an expatriate American writer, I never met Dan Turèll. Let me expound upon that: I once saw and almost met Dan Turèll, in Cykelstalden Café, on the east side of Copenhagen in about 1979-1980. I knew who he was from TV appearances and newspapers and magazines, but he of course did not know me. I sat over a beer there and a plate of hash with a fried egg atop it (*biksemad*), a lunch-time escapee from my office job, wearing suit and tie, and observed the already well-known "Uncle Danny" in his black goatee and signature black Stetson and black suit jacket, his fingernails polished black, drinking a Black Gold Beer and a little glass of black bitter, the only color breaking the black a white shirt and a splashy-colored wide silk necktie. He recognized that I recognized him and nodded in friendly acknowledgment, and I thought, He thinks I'm just any old office stiff in brown suit and brown polyester tie, not a failed writer (which is how I was considering myself then), and what I should do now is leap to my feet and recite Ginsberg's "Howl" or Ferlinghetti's "Autobiography" (maybe just the line that says, "I am only temporarily a tie salesman"), Rexroth's elegy to Dylan Thomas, which culminated, "You killed him./You killed him/In your goddamned Brooks Brothers suit,/You son of a bitch!" But I did not have the moxie to do so. Anyway, what would Turèll have made of that? I ate the rest of my biksemad, brooding about the fact that I was an expatriate writer who had never published anything, although I had tried in the U.S. and Denmark for nearly twenty years. Here once again I had proven myself unworthy to the occasion of seizing an opportunity to meet and speak with a poet who was known to be interested in America and beats and might very well have been open to an approach.

"I've sat many hours at my window and peered down at the street

And watched the lonely men drifting around the sex shops…"

—Dan Turèll, "Life on Isted Street"

Barry arranged a meeting between me and Dan's widow, a Danish poet and actress named Chili Turèll, who was somewhat of a celebrity herself. She owned the copyrights, had bought them back from the Danish Tax Department for a small fortune; Barry suggested that I might be the translator. She agreed to let me try and liked what I did.

Meanwhile, a celebrated documentary filmmaker named Anders Østergaard had just completed a film about Turèll, and Chili saw to it that I was invited to the premiere. The title was *How Short and Strange Life Is*, a line of Dan's long poem—they were all long, Dan needed length to unfold himself—about a last walk through Copenhagen. The film brought the water to my eyes that I had never seized that opportunity, almost three decades before, to meet him.

"Before I die I want to stroll through the city one last time
Let this be my last humble wish
To walk on my own feet through my own city
through the city of Copenhagen
as I've done so many times before
and I'll know this is the last time
and I'll chose my route with care…
thinking how short and strange life is…"

—Dan Turèll, "A Last Walk through the City"

I was still not convinced that I could render into English Dan's poetry. Chili had five years before taken most of Dan's things to Bruun-Rasmussen's auction house to try to get out from under the perception of her as the Ambassador of Dan Turèll and move on. I thought of buying his barber chair. Dan used to sit in that chair "to think thoughts," as the Danes say. I surmised it would be sweet to sit in as a failed poet and think thoughts about Dan, could read his poems in the chair and feel as though

I were having a conversation with his spirit. However, at the auction, the bidding on the barber chair got too rich for my wallet, at ten thousand kroner; then I bid on his black Stetson, but came away from the evening with nothing but an experience of rejuvenated admiration for Dan Turèll and how the Danes loved him.

So I drafted the translations of three poems and sent them to the late Steve Kowit (1940-2015), an American poet whose writing I very much admired and saw akin to Dan's. I did that because I didn't want to make a fool of myself, purporting to render into English the lyrical, musical, Turèllian lines, to subjugate them to a poetry editor's judgement. I was a prose writer, but I felt otherwise when I translated poetry. I felt like a poet, who didn't have to know enjambments, meter, or when a poem began or ended or what was in between. Steve answered me quickly: "Turèll has one of those large, humanistic voices like Mayakovsky or Yevtushenko. Impressive and engaging and at its best hypnotic." (Russians again. But I was reassured that my translations wouldn't embarrass me.)

Unlike the Bolshevik poet Vladimir Mayakovsky (1893-1930), whose life was a decade shorter than Dan Turèll's, perhaps Turèll wanted less to issue a Mayokovsky-style "Slap in the Face of Public Taste" than to reveal to the public the ordinary wonders occurring behind every single window on every single street of every single city.

"...You walk down through a long street
which you know or maybe don't know
in your own city or an unknown one
and you raise your eyes and look at those thousands
of shining lit-up windows
and you know that behind every single window people live
and that simple thought every time is new and strange..."

—Dan Turèll, "Behind Every Single Window"

Equally conversant with Dante and Whitman, Eliot and Pound, Kerouac, Burroughs and Ginsberg, Chandler and Chaplin, Bird and Trane and Webster and Gordon and Lady Day, Presley and Chuck Berry and Lou Reed as well as (like the contemporary American poet, Albert Goldbarth) Donald Duck and Walt Disney, and scores of other European writers, Dan Turèll was nonetheless quintessentially Danish, a student of Copenhagen's streets and serving houses. So much so that a square is named for him in the neighborhood where he grew up; and on what would have been his 60th birthday, another square in the western part of Copenhagen, about which he wrote so movingly, was dubbed "Uncle Danny's Square" for the day. In Copenhagen in 1983, Turèll was host and introduced to a packed audience William S. Burroughs (1914-97) with whom he did not hit it off well and, later, met Allen Ginsberg (1926-97), with whom he did. In an interview by Lars Movin shortly before Ginsberg's death, the Great Beat Poet inquired how Turèll's death had affected the Danish literary scene.

In short, I became the translator of Uncle Danny—his poetry, *Big City Trilogy,* the 400-page masterwork and his breakthrough prose book, *Vangede Pictures* (1975), a down-and-dirty paean to the quarter he grew up in—to supplement my income and to become, laboring over the translations, as near a thing to a poet as I could. This is where the "without permission" in the essay's title comes in: I had permission from Chili to handle Dan's poems, but not Dan's permission.

Nonetheless, I sang with him of Charlie Parker on a west-side street of Copenhagen, of Disney's three little pigs and the Big Wolf's satori, of Danish bodegas, of the east side and the north side and the south harbor and the center of Copenhagen. Charlie Parker is dancing to The Platters' "The Great Pretender" in a west-side Copenhagen bodega, as Bird never did. The four bartenders in "My Old Neighborhood Haunt," taking turns at the stick, "and three of them were always there/the one who was on shift/the one who had just come off shift/and the one who would be on next/and when it was time to change shifts they changed places…" And "Here in our house/many different kinds of people live/ him on the ground floor drinks and his wife goes along too/every night there are arguments in there/every morning they go to work again/and always leave together/in the afternoon they come home and begin all over again/that's how their life is/here in our house" and so on for four or five pages, for every floor and every apartment of the building.

I sang an American approximation of what he sang in Danish, and the spirit of Dan Turèll sang in my ear. I supplemented my income, with the singing, via the Danish Arts Council, but I would have done it for free. My translations of a couple of hundred pages, and essays on Turèll and an interview with Chili were published in *New Letters, Absinthe: New European Writing, Epoch, Poet Lore, Ecotone, Poetry Wales, McNeese Review, Serving House Journal,* and in *American Poetry Review.* Dan's and my bilingual book of poetry was published (without the quotation marks) by Pavillon Press, with four original lithographs, signed by Barry Lereng Wilmont—*Last Walk Through the City/Gennem Byen Sidste Gang.*

The first reading of my translations I did was in 2009 in Underwood Ink, a café on the north side. I was surprised to see there was a full house. Turèll is so esteemed here that Danes flocked to hear him, even in translation. Chili Turèll was present, too, seated quietly at a table in the back, near a window. I read for thirty minutes. I liked the feel of the words, the rhythms, the sound images, the poems, the songs, and felt as though they were in control of my voice. I felt privileged to be transporting these words from the original into another language, and I could feel that the audience was with me. Most people who do public performances know how you can feel that. If there is restlessness, discontent among the audience, it transmits itself through the floorboards up into your own body. I felt no such restlessness.

Then I glanced at Chili in the back. She was looking out the window. While I read, I tried unsuccessfully to interpret the expression on her face. When I had finished reading, Chili rose from her table—a tall, slim, handsome woman with long red hair and an angular face—and crossed the café to me. Her smile had just a touch of sadness to it. She said, "You've given Dan his American voice."

The strange thing was that many people had been skeptical. *You can't translate Dan Turèll,* more than one person had insisted. *He's too Danish!* Yet here was his widow telling me otherwise.

I gave many readings of Turèll in translation—in Copenhagen, in Germany, in England, and in America.

At the start, most of Dan's songs had been taught to me by Halfdan E. Dan Turèll was approached by Halfdan in the year or two before Dan's unexpected death, when there were twenty years between them. Halfdan was in his 20s, Dan in his 40s. Uncertain what he would do with his life, newly graduated from the Royal Music Academy, Halfdan proposed making a CD of Dan's poetry. He would compose the music to it. The CD sold seventy thousand plus copies (huge by Danish standards) in the year before Dan's death, and Halfdan had recorded enough poems that he could make another CD post-Dan. I had listened repeatedly to those two CDs of Dan's poems, read by his initimable voice—Halfdan said Dan's voice was a tenor sax, mine an electric guitar—with Halfdan's music composed to them, supplementing, adding to the lyrics: *Pas på Pengene (Watch Out for Your Money) and Glad I Åbeningstid (Happy in Happy Hour)*.

Halfdan was now a successful movie and TV composer, and I was shy of approaching him, remembering the aborted meeting with Uncle Danny. I was in my 60s, Halfdan in his 40s, the same number of years between us when—though a couple of decades removed—Halfdan had approached Dan. Halfdan had more than sufficient to do; he made Danish movies and TV, had won awards, had a best-selling record and a commission to make a musical tone for the Danish railway system that signaled attention when the railway was to leave or for an important public announcement, a lucrative engagement.

But approach him I did, and he was amenable. He fitted the recording into his spare time, scarce as it was, over four years, and he was ready to mix it in 2013: *Dan Turèll+Halfdan E meets Thomas E. Kennedy: An Introduction.* We launched it that year, the twenty-year anniversary of Dan's untimely death, in Paludan in central Copenhagen, a historic bookstore across the street from the 15th century buildings of Copenhagen University, and at Vangede Library, the home neighborhood in Greater Copenhagen of Dan Turèll and home of the Dan Turèll Collection. Outside the library stands Ken Stilling's enormous sculpture of the alphabet, the D and T enlarged in honor of Dan Turèll. The square on which the sculpture stands is the aforementioned Dan Turèll Square.

In 2014, my speaking voice began to fail, and in 2015, an MR scan showed a large cyst on my brain in the shape of a swimming whale—I nicknamed him "Moby"—pressing on the language center, causing me to lose most of my spoken Danish and English. Not my written English, though, and my ability to translate. The little grey cells are a mystery.

I am extremely grateful that Halfdan accepted my approach affirmatively. I used to have a good reading voice, which was recorded on the CD—right along with Halfdan's music—right before it went. Nothing was spared on the CD: A booklet of 12 of Dan's texts in my translations was included in the folding album cover. Also included were photographs of Dan, Halfdan and me; the renowned artist Thomas Thorhauge did a caricature of Dan on the cover, on the reverse two of Halfdan and me. Translated texts were read by me, the music composed and conducted, recorded and mixed by Halfdan, with Søren Siegumfeldt on alto sax. Sanne Graulund, Susi Hyldgaard, and Lelo Niko sang vocals in the background—one time just a whisper which you have to listen closely for. Jesper Hansen put his and Halfdan's recording company at our disposal, PlantSounds.com.

At seventy-three, I no longer can read aloud, the closest thing to singing I could do. But when I was awarded in 2016—on what would have been Dan Turèll's 70th birthday—the heavy, pure silver Turèll medal (engraved by Barry Lereng Wilmont, using Antonio Pisanello's 14th century technique)—I practiced a written speech many times and delivered it adequately before a large audience. Chili was there, Barry was there, the chair and board members of the Dan Turèll Society were there. My daughter and son-in-law were also there, and my 6-year-old grandson, Leo; he said to his Uncle Daniel, "When Grandfather dies, you inherit the silver medal, and when you die, I inherit the medal, okay?"

Such things are natural, as only a very small child knows.

This award puts me in the club of Hafdan E, Christiania Jazz Club (where I have spent many nights in the company of great jazz), Jakob Martin Strid (intelligent, incisive cartoon author), writers Klaus Lynngaard, Jens Blendstrup, Klaus Høxbro, Marianne Larsen and other artists who have all received the annual Turèll award—and not a moment too soon, before I lost my spoken voice. But I still have the writing ability. I am writing a very long, creative nonfiction novel—and still singing Dan Turèll's American translations. He has provided years of texts with which to occupy myself and supplement my pension, handling another man's poems.

GIVE ME A W!

Robin Parks

In many ways, my sojourn in a tiny community in the Pacific Northwest has been perfect. Then when I meet my husband-to-be, Sean, my life becomes a purgatory of longing: he is in Philadelphia, non-negotiable.

At this point in our lives, neither Sean—who is blind—nor I have enough money for me to simply pack my bags and show up at his doorstep. So while I send off resumes to companies in the greater Philly area, I also consider getting a temporary job until something Back East turns up. Unfortunately, the tiny community where I live boasts the world's tiniest newspaper with the world's briefest classifieds...until one day when Wal*Mart rears its behemoth head.

The newspaper ad is vague, but includes the word "temporary." I am ecstatic: I am nothing if not temporary!

I apply online and within a day get a call from a "recruiter." The recruiter asks me impertinent questions. *Do you do drugs* (he asks this three times)? *Do you have a background in theft? How do you feel about unions?* He asks for the phone numbers of two references.

Never in my working life has anyone ever once actually called a reference, not even when I asked them to. The next day, the recruiter has called both, asking them the same impertinent questions. Then he calls me, and is pleased to report that I have landed an interview. I have no idea what the job actually is.

On a cold spring day, I drive my Festiva to the hotel where the interviews are being held. The Festiva is a tin can on wheels, a zippy little tin can I obtained by providing editorial services to an empty-nester with a memoir-in-the-rough and one too many cars on her hands.

A handful of people mill around the foyer, and little paper signs taped to the walls direct us to rooms off the foyer: "Initial Screening," "First Interview," "Second Interview," "Interview with Management," and finally "Drug Screening." An unsmiling lanky young man offers me a basket of hard candy with a sign hanging from it that reads "Welcome to Walmart."

In the initial screening room—a huge room filled to capacity with desks and facing chairs—the recruiter (I recognize his voice) tells me that my references spoke highly of me, but that I would have to pass a drug test. Then he slides a pile of papers toward me, hands me a pen. I am to fill out the paperwork before I can proceed to the next step. He asks if I have questions.

"What exactly is the job?"

"They'll explain all of that to you in the next step."

He leaves and I fill out the papers, endless "sign here" sheets of tiny type, endless repetitions of my work history, my criminal history. Then comes the personality profile. Page after page of probing philosophical questions, all multiple choice. I check my watch. I have already been here two hours.

When I finish the paperwork, I am directed to wait in the foyer. I watch people come and go, and after a while I am called into another huge room where I queue up behind a long line of people—like at a bank—waiting for an opening at one of the tables. My turn comes and a woman my age beckons me to sit down. Then she gets up and leaves. After a while she comes back, sits down, reads through my paperwork (this takes about 30 minutes), then signs a sheet, tells me to wait out in the lobby, congratulations I made the next interview. Not once does she look me in the eye.

I clear my throat. "What is the job, may I ask?"

"Next!"

By this time it is noon and I am starving, but like a heroin addict, I feel too close to scoring that elusive job description to give up and go home. I eat the candy offered and rub my temples, which are throbbing. After a while, someone calls my name and I enter a narrow room lined with desks and chairs. I am led to one and sit down in front of a middle-aged man who is poring over my paperwork.

"I'd like to ask you some questions," he begins over the din in the room, and proceeds one-by-one through the personality profile. "Why did you answer 'no' to 'should an 18-year-old be jailed for a first-time theft of a $5 bracelet?'"

One by one he calls into question my lefty principles, and one by one I recapitulate until he is satisfied. I tell myself this is acceptable because I am moving on. This is the whole point. This is just moving-on preliminaries. It's all just temporary.

Finally, he gathers up all the papers and stands up. I do, too, then he tells me to sit down. I sit. He leaves.

At last, a tall bearded 30-something wearing a white shirt and tie, the sleeves of his shirt rolled up, sits down in front of me and stares. He has big brown eyes, moist and bloodshot. He has my paperwork, which he does not even glance at. Instead, he opens up a large horizontal file and asks when I can begin.

"Tomorrow," I say, then, "what is the job?"

"Didn't they tell you?" He seems shocked. Then he gets over it, and explains that I will either be on a team inside the store or in the warehouse, which did I prefer?

"The store," I say, having no idea what the hell I am choosing.

"At this point, I would like to offer you employment," he says. "Do you accept?"

"Thank you. Yes. How much does it pay?"

"$7.14 an hour."

I was expecting at least twice that. The company of my fiance will take twice as long to achieve.

"You look shocked," he says.

I smile. I sign. He points me to the drug test room.

A little pale woman my age who looks incredibly tired hands me a kit and a map. I notice her whole body seems to list to the right, as if she is wearing two different heel sizes.

I drive to the medical center where there is a special room for drug tests takers. I feel incredibly guilty, sure remnants of my hippie days still course through my body. I am instructed by a surly nurse to take off my coat and my vest and my shoes before I pee into the specially-marked container. It is dark out by the time I get home.

I get three calls the next day, each verifying one piece or other of my existence, the final call telling me to report to orientation the following day at 8 a.m.

The orientation takes eight hours. The young woman who sits next to me is Latvian, I find out when she has difficulty filling out the 11 forms we are required to sign. It isn't a language barrier, it's that there are not enough pens to go around. There are 60 of us, and 35 pens. *Do you think someone could go out there to the stationery aisle and get us a few more pens?* I almost shriek, but remind myself that each hour I am $7.14 minus taxes closer to my husband-to-be.

Beatrise is gorgeous and baffled. We are instantly friends and raise our hands simultaneously when offered a choice of shifts.

During the next four hours we are subjected to many videos, one of which all but threatens firing if we so much as mouth the word "union." At the lunch break I am depressed enough to warrant spending the day's profits at the Japanese restaurant across the street.

The next day is training day. I arrive at 6:30 a.m. and find Beatrise in the lunchroom, a bandana over her hair, sniffing into a handkerchief. She tells me she is a physicist, but can't get credentialed to teach until she's been here a year. We stare into each other's eyes like deer caught in the headlamps: a whole year at Wal*Mart? She bursts into tears again.

The training begins when the little, pale, tired, listing woman who had given me my drug test kit introduces herself as the HR director. There are about 40 of us crowded into the room, and I cannot hear her over the mumblings of my co-workers. At some point, she leaves the room and we snake behind her, but since the hallway is only two-persons wide, all of her explanations of time clocks, coffee breaks, paperwork, etc., are only heard by the first six people. The rest of us follow silently. We wander through the store, one behind the other, like prisoners, up and down the aisles. I notice the people shopping do not seem to regard this as unusual, a line of 40 people slithering across their paths.

Finally we pool in the middle of women's clothing, and the HR gal appears before us, still talking. I push forward in time to watch her spill something on the floor and mop it up. Behind her I spy Beatrise running through the parking lot.

Back in the lunchroom, the HR director teaches us the codes—blue was especially fascinating since it meant a lost child. All the doors of the vast building instantly lock and we are to converge on the restrooms, where kidnappers take children to change their outfits. Yellow is the code for a hostage situation. She instructs us to faint if a robber tries to take us hostage.

We break for lunch and I again take myself out to Japanese food, swearing to myself and to Sean that I shan't continue this indulgent behavior. In fact, I have begun a mantra—I can do this!—that plays in an endless loop in my head as I dig in to sushi and hot miso soup.

Four more hours of understanding just how dangerous pool chemicals are, just how many square feet of smoking space there are outside, and why-when-where we can park on any given day of the week. At no point in this training do we learn what it is we are hired to do. We are simply told to be clocked in before the time clock registers 8:00 a.m. We are told this is non-negotiable. That this is critical. We are lectured for 30 minutes about this.

The next morning, the line of people waiting to punch in runs from the clock deep into the bowels of the store. I join the line, missing Beatrise's sad presence, and wait with the others. I finally notice that the line is not moving. Someone explains that the clock is jammed and we are waiting for a manager to show up to unjam it. By the time the manager shows up and I get to the clock it is 8:57.

We gather in the same room and finally are told what we will do: move stuff. The 90,000 square feet that is Wal*Mart is going to get reorganized and we are the crack team to do it! Five women and the manager—who the whole time is scratching his crotch—stand in front of us and begin the cheer:

"Give me a W! Give me an A! Give me an L!—"

We are sullen and quiet. They stop the cheer and scream at us to get more involved or the offer of employment will be rescinded.

"Give me a squiggly!" our leaders do the twist and we giggle with embarrassment. The cheer ends with, "What's that spell?" and we shout "Walmart!" and they shout "Whose Walmart?" and we yell "My Walmart" and then they yell something incomprehensible, or perhaps I've just momentarily lost my hearing. Everyone is clapping and woo-hooing and I'm trying very hard not to cry.

The reorganization is going to last six weeks, at which point if we are lucky we will be offered permanent employment. As we are pointed at and chosen for teams, I do the math. Six weeks times five days equals 30 days. At seven bucks an hour, I should be $1,680 closer to Philadelphia and Sean. I can do this!

Pat is my team captain, a Wal*Mart lifer. She's 62, a heavy smoker and when she's not on the reorganizing team, she runs the automotive department, "her" Wal*Mart. She seems very excited about her team: me, a young man and woman, and Ginger, my age, who is a permanent employee. Ginger runs the frozen food section, "her" Wal*Mart, she says with an eyeroll. I love her instantly.

We go out onto the floor and since the new shelving has yet to arrive, we help the other employees do their thing. I end up in pool supplies and am instantly doused with a caustic chemical that eats a hole in my shirt. I run through the 90,000-square-yard scrimmage to get to the bathroom sink. No one seems to notice or care that I am running at full bore holding my shirt out in front of me, crying.

I cannot believe Wal*Mart has reduced me to tears, and I vow not to let this happen again. I am temporary. It is all very, very temporary. I plan to wear the damaged shirt everyday: *See? See this, asshole? Now, leave me alone.*

I spend the rest of Day One helping two women who are clearly good friends. They are both obese, which doesn't seem possible since the work is incredibly physically demanding. We are lifting huge boxes of toilet paper up onto shelves, box after box after box. I'm winded and aching, but they are cheerful and joking. When lunch break comes and I head out to the Festiva for my sandwich, I pass them eating burgers at the McDonald's inside the store.

I sit in the parking lot with the windows rolled down, listening to RVs pull into the lot. I am suddenly overwhelmed with the fact that not only is this my first day, it's only the first half of my first day. So I do more math and decide to face the beast that is Wal*Mart in two-hour increments. The first two hours, then a break, two more hours, then lunch, etc. I can do this!

The next Monday, the manager (as opposed to the associate manager or the assistant manager or supervisor or supervisory assistant) reports on the weekend sales. The numbers are stupendous, in the hundreds of millions of dollars. I can't tell if the manager—who is scratching his crotch the whole time—is reporting on all Wal*Marts or just this one. But it doesn't matter. Either way the amount of money flowing through this world is not to be believed, especially as I look around at my cohorts in our "working" clothes.

After this report, the Crotch Scratcher tells us we have special guests: grad students from the local college who are getting their MBAs. The students and their prof file in and surround us, and I can't help but check their fists for stones. While we all stand there—townies and gownies— Crotch Man tells the students that we are only the temporaries. As they file out, I whisper to each one: "Study hard!"

Monday, week three. After the morning financials—Wal*Mart nets zillions—we have a visitor. The Lions Club president comes in, and Crotcher Dude presents him with a 3x5-foot check for $650 dollars. Someone takes a photo. We do the cheer and go out on the floor.

For the most part, my two-hour increment strategy is working, plus I'm losing about three pounds a day. I've never worked so hard in my life, and I still can't get over how many of the employees (all female) are overweight.

Pat, however, is not. She's all muscle. The shelving has arrived and we proceed to move the entire contents of Wal*Mart from this spot to that spot. We then move this other stuff from that spot and put it in a new spot. We do this hour after hour, stuff after stuff, while periodically a passing manager screams at us.

The shoppers don't seem to notice this chaos. In fact, they don't seem to be aware that they are in a public place. "Shut up, stupid," a woman calls out to her husband. "I hate you, Mom!" a teenager shouts down the aisle.

Pat, clearly Type A, tries to keep her wits about her as the pressure to move more stuff faster builds. We are on the floor, putting metal pegs into metal holes, trying to line up shelves so we can put the stuff on the shelves. Pat is having a hard time keeping track of the holes, so I try to help her. I count out loud, and she whirls around and stops just short of backhanding me in the face. Instead, she opts for yelling, "Shut the fuck up!"

I think about Sean. I think about being a writer. I think about anything other than how close I am to getting hit in the face. The smell of potpourri is overwhelming and I excuse myself, while Pat marches off to have a smoke.

I go to the restroom and hide in the cubicle. That morning I got an email requesting a phone interview. A small Quaker college in the suburbs of Philly wants to talk to me about being their senior writer. It's the day after tomorrow. That's two hours, lunch, two hours, break, two hours. Yo si puedo! I have to call in sick to do the phone interview.

The phone interview goes well, and they invite me to the campus for the full-fledged interview. They will fly me there, put me up in a historic bed and breakfast, take me to dinner at a fine French restaurant, then we will spend the next day interviewing with faculty, administrators, staff, etc. The schedule is such that I will get to be with Sean for a whole evening and part of a day. Oh frabjous day! I count the number of increments: do-able!

My cheerfulness lasts until the next morning, when we are met with a special team flown in from New Orleans. They are taking over the management of the reorganization, because we are doing such a shitty job. Martha, one of the team captains, stands before us and cries, telling us she is tired of working 70 hours a week because of our laziness and how she is humiliated by having to have this new team. She says she plans to retire from Wal*Mart and that we can all fuck ourselves, or something of that nature. Then we do the cheer.

Before I go out to the Festiva for my break, I leave a newspaper on the table. The headline reads: "Walmart discriminates against women, class action suit to be filed." When I return from lunch, the newspaper is gone.

I find the tired, listing HR gal and explain that I have a family medical emergency and must take three days off. She sighs deeply, and hands me a form. I am to gather three signatures from various levels of management. I prowl the arena in search of management. It takes me an hour to get all the signatures. Pat's is not required, though my absence will affect her the most. I decide not to tell her. I'm too scared of her.

For three days I am soaring with joy and excitement. The college campus is gorgeous, the people dignified and brilliant, Sean more beautiful and hilarious than I remembered. I meet future in-laws, eat French food, and explore the gorgeous Pennsylvania spring. Then it's back to Wal*Mart, "my" Wal*Mart.

But I'm filled with hope for the future, and the increments begin to go by more rapidly. For one thing, I am no longer on Pat's team. Ginger and I have joined forces. Ginger is infinitely reasonable and a hard worker. She chats about her kids and her boyfriend and what she watched on TV. She doesn't ask me any questions, which I admire. She has all the physical markings of an unprivileged life: crooked teeth, bad skin, strange hair, cheap clothing. One day, Ginger tells me a story of how a co-worker's boyfriend hit on her, and how disgusted she was by that. She feels sorry for the co-worker, because "she's had a pretty rough life, and she doesn't deserve to be treated like that."

That day there is a terrific crash of broken glass and Ginger and I are assigned to clean it up. It's quitting time, but Ginger continues picking shards of glass off the floor with her bare hands, stacking broken vases into shopping carts. She tells me to go home and I say, "Okay." But I can't do it. Unbelievably, I find myself voluntarily working overtime.

Friday, Week Five, increment two. I'm hanging buttons on pegs when a woman calls out to me to "come on over."

"I'm giving you a Zap card," she says. She pulls a business card out of her red apron and proceeds to write teeny tiny words on it. She hands it to me and says, "I'm on the safety committee, and you hung up that ladder instead of just leaving it on the floor. Good job." I thank her. I read on the card that it is worth one dollar in the vending machines in the break room. I go to the break room and everything in the machines costs $1.25, except gummy bears. I buy them and put them on the table, where they remain for my tenure.

When I get home, there is an email from the college saying close but no cigar. Sean and I have a long chat, and we decide that it is time for me to come to the East Coast, job or no job. I am thrilled, if a little nervous. Sean says he will Fedex me his new credit card. I'll trade up the Festiva for a station wagon, fill it with my stuff, and drive across the states.

On Monday morning, I find the HR gal, whom I now realize is probably 10 years younger than I am. I tell her I am sorry, but I have to move on.

"Oh," she says, "before you go there is another interview."

"An exit interview?"

"No, just one we forgot to do in the beginning. Then after that is the exit interview."

We go into the interview room, sit at a table and the Crotch Yanker comes in. He asks me a bunch of questions—"Can you lift 30 pounds? Are you allergic to pool chemicals? Have you ever shoplifted?"—then leaves. I sit across from the HR gal and ask her if I passed.

Unbelievably, she smiles.

She hands me a piece of paper, the exit interview, already filled out. The last box is marked "yes"—would you hire this person again?

It's good to know I'll always have a job to go back to.

James and the Purple Dungeon

Katie Singer

When I first saw the apartment, I was introduced to a living room of high ceilings and sweeping drapes. I lived at the time in a studio just large enough for my futon to fold out in. This felt like a house, rooms wherever I looked. Antiques, glasses, crystal, velvet, brocade. Those were the words associated with this kind of place, even if I didn't know what all those things were. But the room I ended up working in was like a dungeon, only purple.

James was showing me around; I wondered why he was giving me such an exhaustive tour. It was his guilt, I guess. The way he got the place and all. He wanted to make sure I knew he knew he had a lot even though he seemed to despise it all, to wear it like a cross carried on his back as he trudged the hip streets of Greenwich Village. He stooped even as he fanned his arm within each room, the sunny kitchen, the dramatic sitting room, the dining room from *Pride and Prejudice*, the movie. I was impressed. Not because I really wanted to live like he did or even have what he had. I grew up with all that shit around me and it depressed me. But I was impressed that in New York City one could walk down a sidewalk, peer into an apartment and never really know what lay behind the iron bars and dingy shades of any one window.

So who'd you kill for this place, I asked? It was so not the kind of question I would usually pose. So cliché, like I had never seen nice stuff or high ceilings. But I was trying on different personae at the time and I guess I was experimenting with tough-girl-admiring-yet-judging-other's-indulgent-surroundings right then. It seemed like a clever thing to say mostly because I could think of absolutely nothing else to say to this tall, gaunt, obviously sorrowful man who spoke so quietly I had to hold my breath to hear his words.

I inherited this from my lover. He died last month. Well, didn't I feel like shit. I mean really when a person says he felt like shit, this is what he's talking about. This is putting one's foot in one's mouth, Advanced Placement. I did it so often. I was so awkward, so wrong—so often; wearing the wrong thing, eating the wrong thing, moving in one direction, when all others were heading in the other. So it figured I would finally come to this point. There was no undoing it, no laughing it off. I must say, James' explanation did put everything I saw into a sensible order. The place felt like death. It looked like death. Like maybe Vincent Price was going to appear from behind the red velvet that hung between the dining room and sitting room wearing a black cape and leaning heavily on some kind of ornately carved staff.

A lot of silence ensued. Of course I knew I had to say I was sorry but then was I saying I was sorry about the gaff or the loss or the fact that James may well be ill as well? And what about me? Was I going to catch something? People were dying of AIDS left and right in the city at the time: Keith Haring was a spokes artist for disease awareness; blotched faces appeared behind store counters and in restaurants... People—mostly young men at the time—wore their wounds in public not knowing what else to do. I knew so little. I had some catch words I employed when with the certain crowd that spoke of things like cocktails and Kaposi's Sarcoma. But really I was clueless. Was I going to get AIDS in this mausoleum? Was it really worth working for this guy, making some money under the table just to avoid a few extra hours serving potato skins and beer to yuppies from Wall Street? I quickly decided, yes. Yes it was.

I'm sorry, I said. Hoping it would cover just about everything I did and would do in the event that this poor man actually chose to hire me after my early bout of insensitivity. *So what actually did you want me to do here?* I asked, just to keep things moving forward and so as to avoid time spent on the sorry and all that that entailed. My friend, Gia, had been very sketchy about the details of this job when she first told me about it—something about a shipping business. After I confirmed with her that I would not be down at the docks loading boxes, there was little else she told me. How hard could it be if it was being done in this man's house, I figured. Looking back, it seems a bit risky just to show up to some guy's apartment and offer up my services. But that was how many jobs were gotten in the city back then. There was no time for safety measures and buddy systems—whether it was a paying job or an acting role, you just marched into men's domains and hoped for the best.

James led me downstairs, to the purple dungeon. The basement, if possible, was even more deathly than the upstairs. I learned later that this was due to the fact that his lover died there, died on the bed where months later I would bring James, emaciated now, iced coffees with extra sugar. He could barely drink them, the effort to sip through a straw was too much for his body to make. But these were what we drank together when he was well enough to be my boss. And so goddamit I was going to go around the corner to the deli—no Starbucks there at the time—and get a giant waxed Dixie cup filled with coffee on ice, milk (before my lactose intolerance—everyone's body gives out on them in different ways) and lots and lots of sugar.

The drink run was usually how my days got started at James' on Jane Street. Despite my lack of tact, he hired me on the spot that day. Ironically, his business—which he also inherited from his lover—required a certain sensitive approach but I guess he either thought I had it in me, somewhere, or was just desperate. The business was turning medical supplies into sex toys for homosexual men. Every day, new shipments of rubber tubing, bags, clips and spouts would come to the basement of the Jane Street apartment. Sipping my newfound indulgence of iced coffee, I would stand in the laundry room that abutted the office and begin to unpack and sort the items. Gay men apparently had a lot of imagination, as the things sealed in small bags or coiled round cardboard tubes looked thoroughly unremarkable. But coupled with the right accessory, these items helped give pleasure to gay lovers across the country.

The mail would come in every day, mostly orders handwritten on the flimsy order form we sent out with the simple tri-fold catalog. Everything was presented in a sterile fashion—both literally and figuratively. The catalog contained grainy pictures of the equipment—copied from an official medical supply catalog—with a correlating number alongside each item.

One customer might order six feet of the medium thickness tubing with two enema bags, a clamp and an item that looked somewhat like a kid's telescope, simply called A338. This was the basic set up, but as a custom business we catered to everyone's needs. Some liked more tubing, some liked larger telescopes. Some would send pictures asking if there was any piece of equipment we were familiar with that could do this or that. Then it was my job to scan the medical catalogs we ordered from—no search on the internet back then—and see if I didn't see something that could get the job done.

James and I worked closely together, literally. The office space was located right behind the head of the death bed, the desk where a headboard would normally be. The little space was filled with file cabinets and papers, boxes and tape guns, old photos and headshots. James was an actor. James didn't want to sell sex toys, that was something that fell into his lap so to speak. And out of a sense of duty to his departed lover and because it was easier than waiting tables, James decided to keep the family business going. But his passion was purportedly acting. I had only been in the business a short time myself, but as far as I could tell my boss did not have what it took to be a movie star. For one thing, he was so obviously gay, he would never get a straight man's part. It wasn't that he whooshed when he walked or even talked with a lisp or wore feather boas. The man was just too soft to be straight, his eyes too watery, his lips too full, his physique too slight. Even before the AIDS got him. Nope, he'd be on stage at best his whole life—no money there—performing various renditions of *The Importance of Being Ernest*.

But he had an agent, somehow, and went on auditions which left me alone in the dungeon to do as I pleased. At first I was diligent about filling orders, opening boxes, sorting tubing and the like. But I started to get curious about these guys who ordered stuff. Even though I was an actor and a waitress I wasn't all that close to many gay men. I had no problem with homosexuality, I just wasn't especially interested in it. The only guys I was interested in at the time were ones that might sleep with me. So gay men were a bit of a mystery to me and that is why I started reading the letters they were sending in as opposed to putting them aside for James and going right to the order form.

The letters were both sexy and heartbreaking. The writers sounded lonely and too grateful for a few well-placed clamps and bags. It was as if the business itself, by its existence, was acknowledging them, their lives, and that was what they were most grateful for. And maybe acknowledging it in a subtle, dare I say classy fashion. We were not The Pink Pussycat Boutique, to which I also made deliveries a few times. I dropped off boxes of medical supplies at the large sex shop that used to take up a whole block of Seventh Avenue South. In exchange I received boxes back. I never got to see what was inside those boxes I carried home to James. I wondered if he had found another partner, another lover, someone to share his tired body with as well as his broken heart. Who would risk being with a man whose lover died of AIDS? Or did everyone just risk more back then?

We also sold a little porn pamphlet, a collection of original pornographic tales. Some writer had found himself a niche. I began to read the porn stories. This was not my first experience with porn, I used to read the requisite hidden Playboys when I was a kid, always going right to the sex fantasy columns. Reading the porn pamphlet at James', I was thoroughly drawn in by gay men rhapsodizing on all things homosexual. I was actually turned on. I couldn't believe the idea of two guys could be so sexy. The Polaroids our customers often sent us, in order to show just how great our product was, were not so sexy. But on paper, all this activity sounded hot. So whenever James was off on one of his auditions, I would sit back with my iced coffee and read gay porn. I must have really thought I was getting over on the world: no tables to clear, no customers to appease, no smell of fried food in my hair. Just a cozy little dungeon office replete with sex toys, porn and Jimi Hendrix playing from the radio in the laundry room.

But nothing lasts forever, does it? The first time James called to tell me not to come in I was pissed. I counted on that little bit of money and maybe even more, that focus to my otherwise unruly days. Each morning I would reluctantly wake up, and if I didn't have to cater at the law school, searched *Backstage*—the actor's newspaper—for relevant auditions. After circling each possibility, from cruise ship musicals to East Village children's theatre, I'd go get some breakfast. (Looking back,

181

I probably shouldn't have been getting the extra large corn muffins and cappuccinos because apparently one of my obstacles to fame and fortune was the fact that I was a bit too chunky for the parts I was trying out for. I fell somewhere in between young ingénue and character actor. There wasn't a large call for people who fell in between things in those days.) My days started to wander away from me some time after breakfast as I decided that many of the auditions I circled were never going to pan out. Or I would actually go on a call only to come upon a long, snaking line of actors who all looked exactly the same, holding outdated headshots in their hands, pictures from when they first arrived in New York City, ripe and ready for picking.

So when James started calling somewhat regularly to tell me I didn't need to come in I was incensed. What the hell was I going to do that day? What about my coffee? The porn? Hendrix? I had noticed that James was looking a little more tired of late but I attributed it to the fact that not only was he involuntarily running this business but he was also managing the health care logistics of his very sick estranged brother, the Vietnam vet. Every day he was on the phone or writing letters, sorting through forms and memos and the like trying to get some money from the government to cover all the expenses he and his family were apparently shelling out for the brother. It was a strained relationship the two had and now here James was trying to help this guy who gave him hell his whole life. I told James at one point just to blow the brother off. But James was just too soft to do that.

Now, my boss was a bit prone to drama so the first time I arrived to him in bed, beckoning me to enter with a weak *Come in*, I was having none of it. I spent way too many years looking at my mother in bed like that, too tired to deal with the world she had signed up for. I went out to get us our iced coffees, just like usual. Only later did I notice that the cup remained in exactly the same place I had set it down earlier; beads of condensation rolling slowly down the sides, producing a permanent ring on the black lacquer nightstand.

I continued coming in to work, though intermittently. James told me that business was just a little slow right then. He was a private man and I was grateful for that. Whatever the hell was happening to him,

I didn't want to know about it. I really didn't. I had my own problems. My studio apartment—an indulgent nod to my desperation to live alone in NYC—was becoming an albatross financially. My shoebox of cash never contained enough to make the rent each month. Catering was not reliable; Ken, the manager, ran hot and cold on me and sometimes I wouldn't hear from him for weeks. Then I'd get a desperate call when someone cancelled last minute and I'd be in again—until next time. So I was going through a dry period financially, artistically and romantically. At that moment I was dating an Italian kid whose evil Dad lived in Staten Island and whose foster parents lived in Queens. We spent a lot of our time together on ferries and buses and trains visiting the assorted families in search of money for Rickie, who just couldn't seem to get a job but managed to keep me in jewelry and beer. James' health was the last thing I needed to worry about. I resigned myself to the fact that it was time to start the job search again.

The less I came in to work the more difficult it was when I did. Going through the routine of opening orders and sorting supplies seemed absurd as James lay in bed, his bony fingers barely able to grasp the glass of water he needed to wash down one of his multitude of pills from the sea of vials by his bed. He acted as if this was all temporary but, uneducated as I was, there was a strong sense that he was suffering from something that wasn't planning to reverse itself.

I have always been bad at sickness and death and James spared me much contact with it. Because he was in denial, we worked well together, me calling out questions to him from the office behind his head, he directing me to order more A14s next time. But things were failing: the business, his health, my plans for fame in NYC. I had met a guy while I was tending bar—my most recent new job. He was a doctor, divorced, had a car. He told me he was on his way out of the city, New Jersey maybe. Did I want to come? What the hell I thought. I had no prospects, this was shockingly clear to me. Nothing was flowing the way it was supposed to. Maybe a change of state would be good for me.

As the months wore on and my visits to James grew rarer I realized I was being paid to make sure James was still alive. He must have had friends coming by, there were always flowers or magazines or refills of medicine scattered here and there. One hot summer day, way after we stopped trying to pretend the business was going to continue or that James could hold down iced coffee, I told him I was moving to New Jersey. He smiled a sad, small smile. I felt awful leaving him, knowing I was about to escape something. And that he would not. We never hugged, which was perfect as I wasn't raised to do that sort of thing. We might have touched hands. And I might have even thought about washing right away, just in case. I emptily asked if there was anything I could get for him on what was obviously the last day I would ever see him. I looked past his sunken eyes at the crowded office behind him. Small piles of orders sat on the desk; insurance forms were strewn atop the file cabinet. Bits and pieces of plastic objects lay scattered about the place. It was a freeze frame—it could have been the day I first started but instead it was the day something else was ending. I let myself out of the dark basement and into the sunshine of a summer day in the West Village. Tourists wandered by with maps, kids skipped along with parents on their way back from day camp. Music played from a boom box across the street that was pushed up into the window. I had just left a man to die alone so that I wouldn't have to watch. I headed over to the #1 train at Sheridan Square, unconsciously stopping to get an iced coffee on my way. I was headed back to the apartment to finish packing. I was going to New Jersey, to start my new life. No more medical supplies for me, I would now be with a medical supplier instead. It seemed like a step up at the time.

MY LIFE IN SPANDEX

Michael Aloisi

COPYRIGHT MARTY SALVO. 2006.

My thong was killing me. And I still had another two hours of standing barefoot on the hard linoleum department store floor. Doing my best to see through the white mesh, I looked around, no one was in sight other than my assistant who was snapping her gum and molesting an autograph card; perfect opportunity.

Casually as possible I started to wander from my sanctioned five-foot area. For some unknown reason (okay it's a known reason—stupidity) I was once again set up in an awkward location. Next to the children's clothing, understandably, yet right next to women's lingerie. In fact, if I stretched out my arm too far, my hand would come back with a store brand, 42 DD, tan bra hanging on it. Ignoring this fact, I continued my stroll behind the tiny dresses on the rack behind me. Another quick, hazy look, no one was around. A perfect opportunity to reach behind and try to yank the thong down just a bit. With spandex covering your fingers it isn't always easy to grip things. So it took three solid tries and a few wiggles of my butt to grasp the annoying wad of cloth. One gentle pull alleviated the pressure. As I sighed with relief, a voice startled me.

"Having some problems there?" said a lady older than my own grandmother holding an item of lingerie that I never wanted to picture anyone over fifty wearing. I was busted.

"All part of the job ma'am! Superheroes like me might not have the most comfortable of outfits but they are efficient for crime fighting!" I said in my best heroic joking voice hoping to get a laugh. Instead I got a blank nod as the woman held the see-thru item up to her plump body. Yes, this is the real life of a superhero.

Back on the horribly hard floor (you really start to appreciate carpeting when you have to stand barefoot for four hours at a time on hard surfaces) I felt a bit embarrassed when a little kid off in the distance, no higher than my knee, spotted me in mid-stride and froze. His head tilted on his miniature frame, wondering if I was real. So to prove I was, I waved and said, "Hey pal, come on over here. I'll get you an autograph!" He jumped a bit but I felt it was still safe to approach him. After a while you get a sixth-sense of which kids will freak out and which ones won't. Grabbing an autograph card and marker from my useless, store-appointed assistant, I carefully walked toward the child as a superhero might, holding out the card as a peace offering. This is yet another trick you learn as a superhero—how much a bribe can calm a child. Hand them something colorful and they'll forget they are terrified of you. Ten feet away, things still good. "What's your name buddy?" No answer. I look for his Mom for some help; a reassuring mother is key in situations like this. Of course, she was too busy ignoring her child and instead looking at the $5.99 purses. Five feet away and, Houston we have a problem. His eyebrows were arching in fear. It was too late, it was all over.

"MAAAAAAAAAAAAAAAAAAAA!" The scream wailed out of his tiny mullet hairdo wearing head like a lion's roar. Amazingly, his mother (who actually had the same mullet) turned to her kid and approached us. For a split second I thought she was going to save me and tell little Billy Bob or whatever his name might be, that it was okay. I was wrong.

"Oh, don't be scared. It's just a man wearing a costume. He's not real, he's make believe." It was the dreaded line, the line that breaks the hearts of all superheroes. Being told we are not real, what is this world coming to? Scooping up her kid, she didn't even bother taking the autograph card I was so graciously trying to give him. Instead, she threw him in the cart like a sack of potatoes, stared into my mesh covered eyes and said "You ought to know better than to go around scaring kids like that… why don't you get a real job" before wheeling away leaving her delicate purse selecting duties for another day.

I trudged back to my designated section with her words ringing in my head "why don't you get a real job" over and over again. Part of me wanted to turn around and start an argument with her. What does she know? She's wearing a coffee stained T-shirt shopping in Arkansas at three in the afternoon. Me? I was flown here, put up in the best hotel in town, paid well and I was, well, I was…a guy wearing spandex. Maybe she was right? Maybe at twenty-five I *should* start looking for a real job?

Back in my roped off section (you know to keep the crowds back) it took everything I had to keep my chest high and head up. I was going to hold myself like a real superhero, even if there was no one around. I refuse to break character! I'm proud of my job; at least I kept trying to tell myself that.

"What time is it?" I asked my assistant, who was now attempting origami with my autograph cards. She told me it was three-ten and asked if I wanted a break. I told her, "No, I'm a superhero, we don't need breaks! Do you think the bad guys let us take breaks when we are fighting it out on a roof top?" She didn't find my dedication to my craft impressive, or even funny for that matter.

Less then three hours to go, I told myself, feeling more and more like the man in the Iron Mask. After years of wearing the skin-tight bodysuit, I have gotten used to it. But when you end up standing for hours on your feet, having nothing to do, nothing to even look at, your mind starts to rot. It starts to make up itches that aren't there. Your nose starts to ache from being crushed. You start to blink more, for your lashes actually touch the mesh eyeholes every time you blink. You get thirsty, for there is no way to take the suit off in public for a sip of water. Going to the bathroom? Forget about it! In my head I started to curse the store manager for not getting me a more competent assistant. At least then I could be having a conversation that didn't consist of "You couldn't pay me enough to wear something like that in public." I was miserable. And I knew what was coming next. I only hoped that some kids would show up soon and stop me from arguing with myself in my head. But it was too late.

What am I doing with my life? I'm a writer. Why am I wearing spandex standing, next to women's lingerie in a Wal*Mart in Arkansas? I should be writing right now, I should be making money off of my creativity, not discreetly picking the thong out of my ass behind a rack of clothing. I have had book signings at Barnes & Noble for crying out loud, I shouldn't have to dress *up like someone else for them to want to meet me, I'm somebody dang it!* Then the routine banter in my head turns to the reality of things. *Yes Michael, you may have written things but no one knows who you are yet and you have made about forty cents from your writing. Some day you'll be a famous author but for now, you must make money. And being a superhero pays the bills while giving you the freedom to write. Ah yes, that is why I'm doing this.* Then comes the ego boosting. *Yes, you're in Hicksville today where no one cares about you, but think about what you have done this week alone for crying out loud! You just flew in from closing the New York Stock Exchange yesterday on national TV! The day before that you were in Washington D.C. doing a private party for Senators! And tomorrow you fly to Canada to do a weeklong tour where you know there will be thousands of people in line for you...er, I mean for him.*

After patting myself on the back I was feeling a little bit better, yet I still had more than two-hours to stand there like an idiot waiting for more kids to show up. Looking down one isle I hoped for something exciting to happen. Maybe the store would get robbed and I could stop them. Talk about making the news... *Real Life Superhero Saves the Day, For Real!* It would be a huge media event. Hell—it'd give me a great story to write about some day. But sadly there were no bad guys in sight, just zombie shoppers pulling items off of shelves that they didn't really need. Then off to my left I heard a scream! Could this be it? Finally! "Oh my God!" Spinning my head around I struck a pose, ready to take on the hapless burglar; though I didn't see a masked man or even a shoplifter. Instead I saw two blonde, seven-year-old twins both wearing T-shirts blazing the hero I was portraying and running full speed at me. Their smiling mother was following behind with her shopping cart. Crouching down I prepared myself for the attack of hugs I received. "You're the coolest!" "We watch you every day!" After giving high fives to them and getting their names, their mother finally arrived. "I told you guys I had a big surprise for you today!" She said, pleased with herself for having been able to keep the secret.

The three of us talked for several minutes about "his" movies and how many toys and other hero-related items they owned. Looking at the two hyper kids fighting for my attention, I could see in their identical blue eyes how much they really believed I was the hero they watched everyday.

When I offered them autograph cards, you would have thought I was giving them a million dollars each. They could hardly stop looking at the baseball card sized cards long enough to pose for a picture, in which they both did classic superhero poses, like myself. Putting away her camera the mother asked me "Could you tell Thomas how important it is to take his medicine? Tim doesn't need the medicine, so Thomas thinks he shouldn't either, but I try to tell him he needs to take it." Crouching down to Thomas I quickly made up a story about how when I—well, the hero—was young, I got really sick and wouldn't have gotten better if I hadn't taken my medicine. "And if I didn't get better then, you know what? I wouldn't be able to stop all the bad guys like I do." After elaborating a bit more, I asked Thomas if he would promise me to take his medicine whenever his mother told him to. He agreed and I looked up to see his mother smiling. Then I added "And I'll be calling your mother to make sure you do take it!" The idea of a superhero actually calling their mother made both of them light up with even bigger smiles.

"Well boys, is there anything else you would like to say to me before we leave?" Without hesitation the two once again latched themselves onto my legs for a huge hug. "I love you," the two said in unison before letting go.

Watching them walk away I couldn't help but smile. I didn't save a life or change the world, but I did make some kids happy and hopefully helped make a mother's job a bit easier. That was enough to get me through the next two hours. Even if my thong was riding up again.

About the Authors

Michael Aloisi is a bestselling author, teacher, and publisher whose work has been featured in media outlets around the world. While it's been years since he hung up his spandex, he plans on releasing a memoir of his years as a super-hero in the summer of 2018. Visit http://AuthorMike.com to learn more about his adventures.

Julie Anderson teaches English in Oakland, CA. Her writing has appeared in various journals and anthologies, including *The Gettysburg Review*, *The East Bay Monthly*, *Other Voices*, and *Broad Street Magazine*, which recently nominated her for a Pushcart Prize. You can follow her on Twitter at @julterand.

Renée Ashley is the author of six volumes of poetry: *The View from the Body*; *Because I Am the Shore I Want to Be the Sea*; *Basic Heart*, which won the X.J. Kennedy Poetry Prize; *The Revisionist's Dream*; *The Various Reasons of Light*; and *Salt*, which won the Brittingham Prize in Poetry, as well as a novel, *Someplace Like This*, and two chapbooks, *The Museum of Lost Wings* and *The Verbs of Desiring*. She has received fellowships in both poetry and prose from the New Jersey State Council on the Arts and a fellowship in poetry from the National Endowment of the Arts. A portion of her poem "First Book of the Moon" is included in a permanent installation by the artist Larry Kirkland in Penn Station, NYC.

Kevin Carey is an Assistant Professor in the English Department at Salem State University. He has published three books—a chapbook of fiction, *The Beach People* from Red Bird Chapbooks (2014), and two books of poetry from Cavankerry Press, *The One Fifteen to Penn Station* (2012) and *Jesus Was a Homeboy* (2016). His one-act plays have been staged at The New Works Festival and The New Hampshire Theater Project and his co-written screenplay *Peter's Song* won Best Screenplay at the 2009 New Hampshire Film Festival. Kevin is also a documentary filmmaker. With Mark Hillinghouse he has created documentaries on two poets,

New Jersey's Maria Mazziotti Gillan (*All That Lies Between Us*) in 2012 and *Unburying Malcom Miller*," a Salem, MA, poet in 2017.

Susann Cokal is a novelist, essayist, and professor of creative writing and modern literature at Virginia Commonwealth University, where she also edits *Broad Street Magazine*. Her novels are *Mirabilis, Breath and Bones*, and *The Kingdom of Little Wounds*, which won several honors and awards, including a silver medal in the American Library Association's Michael L. Printz Award series. She has published numerous short stories in journals such as *Electric Lit, Prairie Schooner, Cincinnati Review, The Journal*, and many others. Her scholarly articles range in subject from F. Scott Fitzgerald's narrative code to tuberculosis in Scandinavian novels, as well as hot topics in pop culture such as supermodels, zoos, and the confluence of rhetoric around pornography, nineteenth-century Reformers, and fashions in very private hairstyling. She writes frequently for *The New York Times Book Review* and *Rain Taxi*.

Letisia Cruz is a Cuban-American writer and artist. She lives in Miami, Florida, with her boyfriend and two cats, and currently makes a living as a proposal coordinator for a local engineering firm. She is a graduate of Fairleigh Dickinson University's MFA program and serves as Resident Artist at Petite Hound Press, Online Poetry Re-Features Editor at *The Literary Review*, and Assistant Editor at *Cheap Pop*. Find more of her work at http://lesinfin.com

Walter Cummins is the author of more than 100 short stories. His seven collections are titled *Witness; Where We Live; Local Music; The End of the Circle; The Lost Ones; Habitat: Stories of Bent Realism*, and *Telling Stories: Old & New*. He is also the author of two novels and has published many essays and reviews. His nonfiction books include *The Literary Explorer*, co-written with Thomas E. Kennedy; and a study of the impact of TV on life in the U.S., *Programming Our Lives: Television and American Identity*, co-written with George Gordon. [Author photograph by Minna Proctor.]

Kelly Jean Fitzsimmons is a writer, teacher, and storyteller. Her recent work has appeared in the *Black Fox Literary Magazine, Newtown Literary, Hippocampus Magazine,* and *Hypertext Magazine.* Earning her MFA in Creative Nonfiction from Fairleigh Dickinson University, she also produces No, YOU Tell It!, a "switched-up" storytelling series with a twist: Each NYTI participant develops their own story on the page and then flips scripts with a partner to present each other's story on stage. Learn more and listen to our podcast at http://noyoutellit.com.

Thomas E. Kennedy's forty books include novels, story and essay collections, nonfiction, anthologies, and translations (among them a book of translation of Dan Turèll). Most recent are the four novels of his Copenhagen Quartet (2010-2014) published by Bloomsbury USA and UK: *In the Company of Angels, Falling Sideways, Kerrigan in Copenhagen,* and *Beneath the Neon Egg.* He has published hundreds of stories, novellas, essays, articles, and translations in such magazines and anthologies as the *Pushcart Prize, O. Henry Awards, Best American Magazine Writing, The Best Writing on Writing,* the *New Yorker online, Boston Review, Epoch, New Letters,* and many other periodicals. He lives in Copenhagen and is currently working on a novel, *My Life with Women, Or The Consolation of Jazz.* [Author photograph by Mark Hillringhouse.]

In 2017 **Heather Lang** was voted Las Vegas' Best Local Writer or Poet by the readers of KNPR's *Desert Companion.* Heather holds an MFA in Poetry and Literary Translation, and her poetry and prose have been published by or are forthcoming with *The Normal School, Pleiades,* and *Whiskey Island,* among others. Last year Heather was twice interviewed about her poetry on Nevada Public Radio, and her writing process was on exhibit at the Nevada Humanities Program Gallery. Heather teaches literature and composition part time at Nevada State College, and she serves as a World Literature Editor with *The Literary Review.* Her website is http://heatherlang.cassera.net.

Roisin McLean's essay is her bio. [Author photograph by Thomas E. Kennedy.]

Bill Mesce, Jr. is now a fulltime screenwriting instructor at the University of Maine at Farmington, and is a two-time recipient of the New Jersey State Council on the Arts Individual Artist Grant Award (once for playwrighting, once for prose). His most recent published work includes the Eric Hoffer Award-winning WW II novel *A Cold and Distant Place*, the nonfiction *The Rules of Screenwriting and Why You Should Break Them*, and the contemporary novel *Legacy*.

Robin Parks is the author of *Egg Heaven: Stories* (Shade Mountain Press 2014). Her work has appeared in *Bellingham Review*, *The MacGuffin*, *Prism International*, *Hippocampus*, and other literary journals.

Peter Selgin is the author of *Drowning Lessons*, winner of the 2007 Flannery O'Connor Award for Fiction, *Life Goes to the Movies*, a novel, two books on the craft of fiction, and two children's books. His memoir in essays, *Confessions of a Left-Handed Man: An Artist's Memoir*, was shortlisted for the William Saroyan International Prize for Writing. His novel, *The Water Master*, won the Pirate's Alley William Faulkner Society Prize. Another memoir, *The Inventors*, was published in 2016.

Katie Singer has a Ph.D. in American Studies from Rutgers University-Newark and an MFA in Creative Writing from Fairleigh Dickinson University, where she taught writing, literature, and African-American studies for ten years. She continued her teaching career at Rutgers University while working toward her doctorate in the field of Race, Ethnicity and Modern Society. Her writing consists of short stories, poems, articles, and essays; she has published in various journals and anthologies, most recently in *New Jersey Studies* with a piece on Newark's Krueger-Scott African-American Cultural Center. Katie's most recent creative publication was a short story which appeared in *Influence and Confluence: East and West* in 2016 entitled "Reunification," published by East China Normal University Press.

Per Šmidl is a Danish author. His first novel, published in 1989, was written after he lived for extended periods in France and California. His second novel, *Chop Suey* (1994), became a bestseller. Two years prior to its publication, however, Per Šmidl had left Denmark and settled in Prague following an issue with the Danish authorities. In the thirteen years Per Šmidl spent abroad, he wrote and published four books of prose and a large number of articles. So far his only book in English is the autobiographical novel *Wagon 537 Christiania* published by Serving House Books in 2013. Today Per Šmidl lives in Copenhagen.

Sean Finucane Toner's creative nonfiction has found homes in *The Best of Hippocampus*, the *Best of Philadelphia Stories*, *Brevity*, *Word Riot*, *Ardor*, *Apiary*, *Perigee*, the *Monarch Review*, and at a *Literary Death Match*. Sean has served as the editor-in-chief of *Referential Magazine* and as vice president of the Philadelphia Writers Conference. He has been totally blind since 1995. (www.seantoner.com)

Jayne Thompson teaches English and creative writing at Widener University. She is the director of the Chester Writers House in Chester, PA, a non-profit community writing center. She taught Accelerated Literature at Chester High School for one school year as a special project and has taught in many after-school programs for students as young as eight. In addition, she teaches at a prison in Pennsylvania, S.C.I. Graterford, and recently published an anthology of writings geared towards young people with her incarcerated students. Serving House Books published *Letters to My Younger Self: An Anthology of Writings by Incarcerated Men at S.C.I. Graterford and a Writing Workbook* in 2014. All profits from the book go toward providing free copies to young people at juvenile detention facilities and high schools where she offers writing workshops. She is working on a second anthology that gathers the voices of incarcerated women.

www.ingramcontent.com/pod-product-compliance
Lightning Source LLC
Chambersburg PA
CBHW051256250626
47155CB00009B/3311